31 Day Devotional for the Brokenhearted

A Devotion a Day to Heal Your Hurting Heart

Alicia Cummings

Copyright © 2024 by Alicia Cummings

All rights reserved.

No portion of this book may be reproduced in any form without written permission from the publisher or author, except as permitted by U.S. copyright law.

This publication is designed to provide accurate and authoritative information in regard to the subject matter covered. It is sold with the understanding that neither the author nor the publisher is engaged in rendering legal, investment, accounting or other professional services. While the publisher and author have used their best efforts in preparing this book, they make no representations or warranties with respect to the accuracy or completeness of the contents of this book and specifically disclaim any implied warranties of merchantability or fitness for a particular purpose. No warranty may be created or extended by sales representatives or written sales materials. The advice and strategies contained herein may not be suitable for your situation. You should consult with a professional when appropriate. Neither the publisher nor the author shall be liable for any loss of profit or any other commercial damages, including but not limited to special, incidental, consequential, personal, or other damages.

Unless otherwise noted, all Scripture quotations are from the New King James Version of the Bible. Copyright © 1979, 1980, 1982 by Thomas Nelson, Inc., publishers. Used by permission.

Scripture quotations marked NIV are from the Holy Bible, New International Version. Copyright © 1973, 1978, 1984, International Bible Society. Used by permission.

Scripture quotations marked CSB are taken from the Christian Standard Bible®, Copyright © 2017 by Holman Bible Publishers. Used by permission. Christian Standard Bible® and CSB® are federally registered trademarks of Holman Bible Publishers.

Scripture quotations marked ESV are taken from the ESV Bible® (The Holy Bible, English Standard Version®) copyright © 2001 by Crossway Bibles, a publishing

31 DAY DEVOTIONAL FOR THE BROKENHEARTED

ministry of Good News Publishers. Used by permission. All rights reserved.

Written by: Alicia Cummings
Cover Design by: Alicia Cummings

ISBN: 979-8-9878216-2-6 (Ebook)
ISBN: 979-8-9878216-3-3 (Paperback)

A Letter to My Brothers and Sisters

Dear friends,

I see you. God sees you. I know the pain you are going through. I have faced heartbreak many times in my life. Most of them were masked with alcohol, traveling, dating apps, and staying busy with friends – AKA masking my broken heart in all the wrong places – the devil's method. Being still terrified me. I didn't want to feel the broken parts of myself. I didn't want to accept the loss of losing someone for fear of being alone. As a result, I clung to people longer than I should have when God was really wanting me to let go.

I knew things needed to change when I faced my last heartbreak, which happened most recently when I began writing this book. I was tired of feeling stuck and wanted to be healed for real this time. Instead of relying on other things I mentioned above to escape my pain, as I used to do before, I tried something different. I chose to do it God's way instead of the devil's.

Once I gave God my commitment, He rescued me and healed me in such a way that I could never go back to my old ways of doing things. The 31 verses in this devotional helped me through my healing process, and I hope they can do the same for you. As I clung to these verses and stood on God's Word, they transformed my life. I wrote this devotional to encourage those who are going through what I once experienced. Let these daily devotions speak to you and bring healing to your heart.

LET'S PRAY

Dear Heavenly Father, as my brother or sister embarks on this journey over the next 31 days, I pray that You speak to them through these daily devotions. May Your Word penetrate their souls and bring healing to their hearts. I pray that my words will bless Your children and bring them to a place of peace. Lord, I ask that You manifest Yourself in their lives over the next 31 days so they can feel Your presence. Make Yourself known to them, and reveal Your glory to them. I pray that You bring complete restoration to their lives. In Jesus' name, Amen.

*Weeping may endure for a night,
But joy comes in the morning.*

Psalm 30:5

How This Devotional Will Work

- There are 31 devotionals – one to be read each day.

- There is a journaling and prayer aspect for each daily devotion. You will need a separate blank journal to respond to the journaling questions, and write down your prayer requests to God. WRITING IT DOWN is essential.

- Circle your prayer requests from that day, and when God answers it, come back to it and check it off with the date it was answered.

- Write down all the ways God spoke to you from that day. This is why journaling is so crucial - it helps you keep track.

- After you complete the 31 days, go back and look at what you wrote for each day, and track your transformation. You will appreciate these to look back on one day.

Contents

1. Day 1: God Has a Plan for You — 1
2. Day 2: God is Near — 5
3. Day 3: God Promises Rest — 9
4. Day 4: God's Ultimate Purpose — 13
5. Day 5: Hope in the Future — 19
6. Day 6: Strength Through the Suffering — 23
7. Day 7: God Is Your Anchor — 27
8. Day 8: God Is Your Defender — 31
9. Day 9: It's Not Forever — 35
10. Day 10: Overcoming Fear — 39
11. Day 11: God's Purpose in Our Pain — 43
12. Day 12: God Is the Provider — 47
13. Day 13: Leave It to God — 51

14.	Day 14: Comfort in God's Presence	55
15.	Day 15: Trusting God in the Unknown	59
16.	Day 16: Give It to God	63
17.	Day 17: God Is the Healer	67
18.	Day 18: God Will Restore You	73
19.	Day 19: No Prayer is Off Limits	77
20.	Day 20: A Fresh Start	83
21.	Day 21: The Bigger Picture	89
22.	Day 22: More than Enough	95
23.	Day 23: Waiting on God	99
24.	Day 24: Strength for a Weary Soul	103
25.	Day 25: It Will All Be Worth it	107
26.	Day 26: Faith in the Unseen	113
27.	Day 27: Focus on God	117
28.	Day 28: A Changed Heart	123
29.	Day 29: It Will All Make Sense	127
30.	Day 30: God Will Finish the Work in You	133
31.	Day 31: God is for You	139
	About the Author	143

Day 1: God Has a Plan for You

For I know the plans I have for you," declares the Lord, "plans to prosper you and not to harm you, plans to give you hope and a future. - Jeremiah 29:11 NIV

This verse holds a special place in my heart. When I was going through a traumatic breakup from a toxic relationship, this was one of the very first verses God kept showing me. This verse comforted me when everything around me was crumbling down. So many things were up in the air. *Where would I live? Is God directing a career change? How do I handle these financial problems? How will I figure all this out during this intense breakup?* But through all of the instability, this verse eased my anxiety.

Months after my breakup, I started sharing my journey on social media to help others heal from toxic relationships. A lady I didn't know commented on one of my videos with this exact Bible verse, Jeremiah 29:11. During this time, I had just started getting closer to God and growing in my relationship with Him. Two days later, I was staying in an Airbnb because when I got home from being out of town, it looked like someone had broken into my house, so I booked an Airbnb to be safe. God planned it to happen that way because, in this Airbnb, there were bookshelves filled with Bibles and all kinds of books about Jesus. That is when I first started reading the Bible. God set that up on purpose.

As I walked downstairs in the Airbnb to go to bed that night, I passed this toy sailboat sitting on a bookshelf. As I got closer to see what it said on it, I noticed it was the Jeremiah 29:11 verse. I started laughing and crying at the same time. Through this verse, God was speaking to me to remind me that He knows the plans He has for me and that I didn't need to worry or try to figure it all out. God used a sailboat on a bookshelf to encourage me. When you realize that nothing is ever a coincidence when it comes to God, you start to see purpose in everything. God will be your captain and steer you where you should go.

A few days later, I was in line at a coffee shop and was frustrated that the line was so long. As I stood in line waiting, I saw a girl's computer screen that caught my eye. She had the Jeremiah 29:11 verse as her computer background. God is so strategic and funny. Here I was, impatiently waiting in line when all God was trying to do was speak to me.

God orchestrates the events in our lives for His purpose. Let this verse give you the comfort you need, knowing that God is in charge and His plans for you are good, even when you don't understand. Sometimes, God takes us on a detour to a place we would have never gone to on our own so that His plans for us can prosper. Just like how God redirected me to that Airbnb, it led me to start reading the Bible off a bookshelf in a house I wasn't even supposed to be at. God had a plan all along.

Trusting God in a season of unpredictability can make us feel out of control. We don't like being out of control or not knowing what the future looks like, but this is where God wants us to surrender. Our insecurity can breed a dangerous distrust towards the Father. God has good plans for you, as His Word says. All we must do is yield to the Holy Spirit's leading. If God is pulling you to or from somewhere, trust Him - even if it's to a random Airbnb like He did to me. I can only imagine how different my life would be right now had I not been in that Airbnb that inspired me to read the Bible. Even when you don't understand and it doesn't make sense, trust that God is still leading you.

REFLECT/JOURNAL

What area in your life can you surrender more to God? Ask God to reveal any areas where you need to let go of control. Write this verse down and meditate on it until you have memorized it. Be attentive to when this verse shows up, as it may be God confirming His Word to you. Write down each time it appears so you can revisit them and see how God spoke to you through this verse. Trust me, it will happen.

PRAYER

Dear Heavenly Father, thank You for the good plans You have for me. Help me to trust You with my future and surrender the anxiety and worries I have. Thank You for giving me hope in the unknown. Lord, as I go about my day and week, remind me of Jeremiah 29:11 by showing this verse to me so I can be encouraged to know You are speaking to me. I trust that You are guiding me every step of the way, even when I don't understand. In Jesus' name, Amen.

Day 2: God is Near

The Lord is close to the brokenhearted and saves those who are crushed in spirit. - Psalm 34:18 NIV

When our heart hurts, it can make us feel isolated, numb, and tired. But in these moments of despair, God draws closer to us. He is not a distant observer, but a compassionate Father who feels the pain we feel. He is near to us when we feel like giving up, offering a source of strength that can empower us. Through my breakup, I felt God's presence more than ever. Even when I felt alone, God gave me peace, knowing He was always with me. His constant presence, even in the darkest times, can bring reassurance and comfort. Emotional pain can affect us physically, causing actual pain in our hearts. Yet, with God's strength, we can endure the afflictions we face, finding hope in His power.

Heartbreak can feel intense because we now have a void in our hearts of what we once thought we should have. We are left with a gaping hole we don't know how to fill. Psalm 34:18 reminds us that God's love and presence can comfort us during heartbreak. He is near when we are crushed in spirit. He is always available to us, especially when we are suffering and going through difficult times. It can be hard to receive God's comfort under difficult circumstances when all we want is a quick fix for our pain. God wants to draw near to you and hear from you. Talk to God as you would to your best friend or someone you feel comfortable with. Tell Him exactly how you feel and what's on your mind. God's comfort and peace are always accessible to us when we come to Him in prayer.

It can be hard to be vulnerable with God when you're in pain, but God already knows how you feel. When you are honest with God with your emotions, it allows Him the opportunity to heal you. God can't fill a void you try to avoid. He can't heal who you pretend to be; He can only heal you when you come to Him broken and ask Him for help. God cares about your feelings and wants to have a conversation with you. Allow Him in so He can heal your broken heart.

When Jesus healed the man with the withered hand in Matthew 12:10-13, he had to take action and stretch out his withered hand to be restored. When Jesus said to him, "Stretch out your hand," the man stretched out his withered hand, taking advantage of the opportunity for his hand to be healed. He could have easily stretched out his good hand in fear of embarrassment or shame and missed out on his healing miracle. We, too, must come to God unashamed with the withered parts of us so He can heal us.

I remember every night and every morning crying out to God, asking Him to heal me and help me through my pain. I didn't want to numb or try to avoid the pain like I always did in the past. I wanted this time to be different and for God to really heal me. Once I was vulnerable with God and desperate for relief, He showed up. He gave me the strength I needed to get through each day. Every day became more manageable because I knew God was with me. I always felt like I had a friend with me because I turned every moment into a conversation with God.

God wants an ongoing relationship with you. The Lord hears when we cry out to Him and rescues us from our troubles. Even when it seems unbearable, God is waiting for you to call out to Him for help. Satan wants to use your grief to isolate you from God, but God wants to draw you closer through your pain. Many turn away from God during difficult times, but God is always by your side, cheering you on. All we must do is call on Him for help.

REFLECT/JOURNAL

How have you felt God's presence through your pain? Ask God to help you feel His presence. Write down all the little moments you have felt Him close to you. Do you hide your brokenness from God, or are you exposing the withered parts of yourself for Him to heal?

PRAYER

Dear Heavenly Father, I need You. Please help me lean on You for comfort and strength during this season of pain. My heart is hurting, and sometimes I can't feel Your presence. Remind me that You are near to me and hear my cry for help. Help me to open my heart to receive Your love and peace. Father, remind me that You care about everything I go through and can heal my pain even when it seems impossible. I trust that You will get me through this heartbreak. In Jesus' name, Amen.

Day 3: God Promises Rest

"Come to me, all you who are weary and burdened, and I will give you rest. - Matthew 11:28 NIV

Going through any heartbreak can be draining and exhausting. Your soul feels heavy, and your body feels weak. God promises to give you rest. This verse is an invitation from Jesus inviting all of those who are weary and burdened to come to Him. We can rest easy knowing that we are not alone and can surrender our burdens and worries to God. Throughout life, there are times when we carry way too much. Not only do we carry the weight of our own burdens, but many times, we also carry the burdens of others.

When Jesus says, "Come to me," it is an open invitation to take the weight off our shoulders and give it to Him. He wants to take the load off of us and carry it for us. That is why He died on the cross for our sins to free us from our burdens. Jesus calls us to come to Him to relieve our needs instead of doing things in our own strength. In our own might, it can feel unbearable, but with Jesus, it can be easy and light.

God is fighting our battles on our behalf even when we can't see or feel it. We are not meant to fight our own battles. Even when we feel like we've hit rock bottom, God is waiting at the bottom, ready to lift us back up. Meditate on this verse and repeat it in your head that God promises to give you rest. I saw a quote once that said, "Sometimes God lets you hit rock bottom so that you realize He is the rock at the bottom." How good is that? That couldn't be more true. Sometimes, God lets us hit rock bottom so we can realize He is the only one to pick us back up.

I remember going through my traumatic breakup, where I would wake up already feeling exhausted and drained before even getting out of bed. The days dragged on forever, and sleeping was nearly impossible. One of the things I did that helped me rest in God's comfort and peace was sleeping with my Bible in my bed. Even when I felt alone and emotionally drained, having my Bible always next to me made me feel safe and that God was with me and protecting me. Doing that also eased my anxiety and helped me sleep.

I had intense nightmares after my breakup, and sleeping with my Bible open to Psalm 91 significantly helped my nightmares subside. I now know those nightmares were from the devil because he knew I was getting closer to God in this breakup. This is what is known as spiritual warfare. The devil hates when we get closer to God, so he will try to stop it in any way he can.

Another thing that prevents us from coming to God for help is our pride. Our pride can get in the way of thinking we can handle it on our own and figure it out all by ourselves. Thinking this way can block us from receiving the true peace God wants to give us. He is waiting for us to come to Him with arms wide open. We are not strong enough to bear all the weight of our everyday burdens and aren't meant to. God didn't make us strong enough to handle it all on our own. We are weak on our own, but with God's strength, we can do all things through Him.

REFLECT/JOURNAL

How are the burdens of your heartbreak weighing you down? Are you trying to bear it alone, or have you given it to God? Have an honest conversation with Him and express what is weighing you down. Ask Him to take the burden from you and give you the strength to carry it. He understands the depth of your pain and knows what you need. Allow Him to be the Father you need and take away your pain, just like a parent who wants to ease their child's suffering. If you let Him, God will do the same for you.

PRAYER

Dear Heavenly Father, thank You for letting me come to You with my burdens and for giving me rest when I am weary and exhausted. Sometimes, I carry too much and feel emotionally drained. Help me take off the weight and give it to you. Show me how to rest, knowing You have everything under control. Help me worry less, and let me find rest in You. In Jesus' name, Amen.

Day 4: God's Ultimate Purpose

We know that all things work together for the good of those who love God, who are called according to his purpose. - Romans 8:28 CSB

Romans 8:28 is one of my favorite verses. It comforts me to know that God will use even the bad parts of our story and our past and turn it around for our good and His glory. Before I was saved, I was deep into New Age beliefs and practices. I traveled all around the world, seeking out these mystical experiences and spiritual transformations. I wanted to have these deep spiritual experiences that people talked about. Little did I know, my soul was actually craving the Holy Spirit. New Age spirituality is just a demonic counterfeit of the Holy Spirit.

When I was in the New Age, I thought I could create my own reality by meditating and thinking positively. My morning routine consisted of meditating, journaling what I was trying to manifest using the law of attraction, and raising my vibration by listening to high-frequency music. I did this for five-plus years until I traveled to Bali to heal after my breakup to seek out these New Age healing practices, and this is where God revealed the truth to me about these practices.

I always believed in God but had no idea that practicing New Age was against the Bible until Jesus met me on my bathroom floor the last day I was in Bali and saved me. He gave me divine revelation at that moment, and suddenly, my eyes were opened to the truth. I had never read the Bible before then, so I didn't know the truth. The enemy's lies and deception blinded me to the truth.

Right after I returned to the States from Bali, God put a hunger inside of me to read the Bible and know His Word. God used all of this for my good because now I am in full-time ministry evangelizing on social media and exposing New Age deception, opening many people's eyes to the truth. God turned my mess into a message and my test into a testimony. God uses everything for our good so that we can help others and bring glory to Him.

When I was in the worst toxic relationship of my life, filled with abuse, lies, cheating, and lots of sin, I was so far away from God. All of my time was consumed in the toxic relationship I was in, and I had made it an idol. One night, I cried out to God, begging Him to get me out of that relationship, and the next day, He did exactly that. Months later, He put it on my heart to write a book to help others leave and heal from a toxic relationship. In my first book, *Better Days After a Toxic Relationship*, I shared how God gave me supernatural strength to leave that toxic relationship and heal in a godly way, putting all my trust in God's plan. God used even my rock bottom for my good and for His glory. He used every part of my story and turned it into something good.

The trials we face can seem debilitating in the moment, but God can use even the setbacks and turn them around for good. I have seen God turn my lowest moments into something good. It might not happen immediately, but Romans 8:28 is a promise we can stand on. I know it's hard to believe this when you're going through it, but God has a bigger plan, and you can trust in that because His Word says it. God will use every broken piece of your story and restore it for His ultimate purpose. Trust in that promise.

God uses everything - our suffering, the setbacks, the heartbreak, our messy past - for our good. Even the wrong decisions and wrong turns you have made, God can use all of it. Nothing from your past is too messed up or too far gone for God to use. God will use your setbacks and your story to bless others. Everything that you went through wasn't for nothing. Nothing is a waste when it comes to God. He uses every shattered piece, puts it back together, and restores it to make it whole again.

I wonder how often we carry the shame and guilt from our

past failures. God can turn that very same thing into wisdom and a testimony to help others who might be going through the same setbacks we experienced. It will all make sense in reverse. It's hard to see how the trials we face now can turn into something good, but later, we can look back and see how God worked it all together. The setbacks we face have a purpose.

Sometimes, God allows setbacks to strengthen our faith so we can learn to depend on Him. If it weren't for that toxic relationship I endured, I would have never given my life to God. God used that very same thing to draw me closer to Him. Every time you feel overwhelmed and defeated by your circumstances, remind yourself of the promise of Romans 8:28.

REFLECT/JOURNAL

Can you look back on past moments and see how God used it all for your good? How has it shaped and molded you into who you are now? What were the defining moments in your life that God used to elevate you? You could be in a defining moment right now from this heartbreak and don't even know it. Ask God to show you what this setback is teaching you.

PRAYER

Dear Heavenly Father, You promise in Your Word that You work all things together for my good. I am overwhelmed with the pain of my heartbreak, and it's hard to see a way out. God, help me to remember You have a purpose in my pain. Even though I don't understand, give me Your peace and comfort to focus on Your faithfulness. Even when things seem hopeless, I know You are working it all together for my good. I know Your ways are better than mine. In Jesus' name, Amen.

Day 5: Hope in the Future

For I consider that the sufferings of this present time are not worth comparing with the glory that is going to be revealed to us. - Romans 8:18 CSB

We all face seasons of suffering in life. It is inevitable. But God promises us that the suffering we face is not worth comparing with the glory that will come after. I've experienced many trials and tribulations throughout my life, starting from an early age with my parent's divorce and not growing up with a father. I've had many failed businesses and failed relationships. I went from one toxic relationship to the next, where I experienced physical and emotional abuse over a decade since I was 16 years old. I struggled in the relationship department because I was trying to fill a void from my father.

I couldn't seem to get anything right. From the outside, it looked like I lived the perfect life. I was traveling the world, posting the best parts of my life all over social media while secretly battling with severe depression and anxiety. I pretended to have it all together on the outside while feeling like I was dying on the inside. During the months of my healing process, the verse Romans 8:18 kept popping up, and it really spoke to and encouraged me. I clung to this verse because it gave me hope to know that what I'm currently going through is only temporary and doesn't compare to what's ahead.

Apostle Paul, who had experienced more suffering than most of us today, wrote Romans 8:18. Yet he says that the future glory will far outweigh the current sufferings. The glory that will be revealed to us won't even be comparable. Embracing suffering is not easy, but there is always a purpose in it. During seasons of heartbreak and pain, we have to trust God more. We have to believe that what He says in His Word is true. We must lean into God's truth even more when we become hopeless and doubtful.

I can look back at all the times I endured suffering and see how God's hand was in all of it. The amount of wisdom I gained from all the lessons taught me how to have discernment for future situations. God stretched my faith and taught me that even my failed businesses had a purpose in His plan. Each business venture and job that failed taught me the lessons and skills I would need to later run a business and ministry for God's Kingdom.

Every season of your life has a purpose. God will use situations in your life to give you the wisdom and skills you need for the next season. The heartbreak in your life has a purpose. You're one step closer to the one God has for you. Before God gives us the person He has for us, He uses our experiences to shape and mold us. God uses heartbreak to refine us. Each relationship teaches us something and better prepares us for the next relationship. Don't see this heartbreak as a failure; see it as one step closer to the person God has for you.

God is a good Father and wants the absolute best for His children. He doesn't want us to suffer, but sometimes suffering is necessary for our growth so God can take us where we need to go. We learn valuable lessons and wisdom from our sufferings that we wouldn't have otherwise learned without them. Through the setbacks, we get stronger, and our faith increases because we see God's faithfulness come through. God will never leave you nor forsake you. I can testify that God has repeatedly gotten me out of messy situations and put me back on my feet. He never left me where He found me.

God loves to do the impossible. He loves when we have childlike faith in Him when our situation looks and feels impossible. God will bring you out of your pain, and I can confidently say that because I've seen Him do it repeatedly for me. Sometimes, God allows things to happen to build up our faith. I know heartbreak can feel suffocating, but ask God to minister to you while you re-read this devotional. Ask Him to speak life into your situation and give you a fresh perspective. I can promise you that the pain you feel right now is only temporary, and you can surrender your future and put it in

God's hands.

REFLECT/JOURNAL

What lessons have you learned from this past relationship? How will the wisdom you've gained help you in your next relationship? Can you see what has failed in your past (relationships, jobs, decisions, etc) been used to benefit you in your future? Reflect and look back on the things that seemed painful back then and how it turned out to be a blessing.

PRAYER

Dear Heavenly Father, I trust You even when it hurts. Please help me to endure the suffering I am going through with joy, knowing it is only temporary. Lord, give me the strength to get through my pain and sorrow. Help give me hope and remind me that You have good plans for me. May You give me the courage to push through and not give up. In Jesus' name, Amen.

Day 6: Strength Through the Suffering

I can do all things through Christ who strengthens me. - Philippians 4:13 NKJV

Two months after my breakup, I was working at a coffee shop and felt a sadness come over me. At that moment, this guy walked right by me and sat down at the table in front of me with a shirt on that said *Philippians 4:13*. At that time, I hadn't memorized any Bible verses since I was new to reading the Bible, but I looked it up, hoping that it would speak to me. Reading the verse instantly brought me comfort, and I knew God was speaking to me through this verse. It reminded me that He was with me and that His strength could get me through the difficult days.

Philippians 4:13 was a verse I continuously spoke over myself every day when I felt weak and defeated. I wrote it down in my journals, on sticky notes on my wall, and constantly repeated it in my head. Meditating on this verse helped me overcome the enemy's lies of thinking I couldn't get through it. This verse tells us we can do *all* things through Christ who strengthens us. This verse is humbling because it reminds us we are not in control; God is. All things are possible with God. Even when I felt like my heart couldn't take any more pain and that I couldn't cry any more tears, this verse comforted me and reminded me of the strength I have through Christ.

When we are tested with trials and suffering, God can give us supernatural strength to endure our hardships. I look back and wonder how I survived so much pain, and the only reason why I'm still here today is through God's supernatural strength. When things don't go our way, it can be easy to lose our faith and trust in God, but this is where He teaches us to fully surrender and depend on Him. The good news is that God promises to give us strength through difficult times.

When you are hurting, praying and seeking God may be the last thing on your mind. You wish you could fast-forward and not feel the pain anymore. But I promise you, God is with you in the pain. I know it can be hard to trust that God has a plan through it, but this is when you need to surrender even more to Him. We are weak on our own, but God gives us the strength to endure our challenges.

Being content is difficult, especially when you're in pain and relying on God to fulfill your needs. True contentment in a difficult season can only be found in the strength of Christ. Your own strength may falter, but God's strength is unwavering.

Write this verse on a sticky note, on your mirror, or set it as your phone's lock screen to remind yourself that you can persevere through God's strength. Reflect and meditate on this verse daily, and let it bring you comfort. Pray and ask God to empower you to overcome; He will.

REFLECT/JOURNAL

Write God a letter and tell Him what You need and where you are struggling. Tell Him where you feel weak and how you need His strength to overcome it. For example, I needed God's strength to avoid texting my ex or respond to calls, emails, etc. I would repeat this verse out loud to myself whenever I noticed myself feeling weak and vulnerable again. Ask God to help you stay strong.

PRAYER

Dear Heavenly Father, teach me to look to You for strength and not to rely on my own willpower. Lord, thank You that I can do all things through You. When I get sad, please help me remember I can bring my worries to You. I pray that You give me the strength and courage I need to get through each day. Help me to trust in You even when it's hard. In Jesus' name, Amen.

Day 7: God Is Your Anchor

So do not fear, for I am with you; do not be dismayed, for I am your God. I will strengthen you and help you; I will uphold you with my righteous right hand. - Isaiah 41:10 NIV

We can feel so alone when our world is crashing down. Sometimes, it can feel like God isn't with or listening to us. During my season of heartbreak, I felt like I was thrown into the deep without an anchor. I felt like I was flopping around, trying not to drown. Every day, keeping my head above water seemed like a struggle. That's how you might be feeling right now. You might feel like you only have an anchor when things are calm or going your way, but when the waves get choppy, you lose the anchor, and your emotions feel out of control.

God is the calm in the storm. Allow God to be your anchor when you have nothing else to cling to. Isaiah 41:10 assures us to fear not, for God's help is always present. We are never alone because God declares, "Fear not, for I am with you." God promises to strengthen us and help us. Just like an anchor that stabilizes a boat in the ocean, God is the anchor that supports us even in the most violent of storms. God is a reliable anchor for our souls, no matter how turbulent it becomes.

In times of pressure or when confronted with problems, it's easy to lose faith and succumb to fear. However, God calls us to keep our eyes on Him and trust in His power. When Jesus called Peter to step out of the boat, Peter began to walk on the water. But when Peter focused on the storm, he became afraid and started to sink. He cried out, asking Jesus to save him. Matthew 14:31 says, "Immediately Jesus reached out his hand, caught hold of him, and said to him, "You of little faith, why did you doubt?" This story reminds us of the importance of maintaining faith during challenges, empowering us to stay strong and resilient.

Take note of how the Bible states, "Immediately, Jesus reached out his hand" when Peter called out for help. The word 'immediately' is significant here. It signifies that God is swift to respond when we start to sink and call out to Him. Our focus should remain on Him, undeterred by the storm raging around us. In our pain, God is our fortress. He is our stabilizer. If we attempt to rely on our own strength, our suffering may only deepen our worry and anxiety. However, when we keep our eyes fixed on Jesus, He will rescue us from sinking.

Peter only started to sink because he took his eyes off Jesus and started looking around, panicking because of his circumstances. Peter forgot that Jesus had all the power in the world to protect him from the storm and strong winds he feared. Jesus allowed Peter to sink for a moment but didn't let him drown. Jesus allowed this so Peter would know not to rely on himself but to look to Jesus for help. Many of us look like Peter when we panic in the middle of a storm. We forget that God is in control and that our strength and help comes from Him. We don't have to fear our circumstances if we truly believe God is our anchor.

REFLECT/JOURNAL

Peter only started to sink when fear and doubt overtook his mind, but Jesus asked him why he had such little faith. You might be in the middle of a storm right now, but your faith is what will keep you afloat. What area of your life is it hard to trust God in? Do you believe He is the anchor in your situation? What makes you feel out of control right now? Can you surrender your emotions to God and trust Him even though it looks rough?

PRAYER

Dear Heavenly Father, thank You for being my anchor. I put all my hope and trust in You. Please help me to keep my eyes focused on You and not my circumstances. Lord, my life feels all over the place right now, and I struggle with the pain of losing someone. God, help me to ease my fear and anxiety and give me the strength to get through this. When I start to doubt or lose hope, may You remind me that You are my anchor. In Jesus' name, Amen.

Day 8: God Is Your Defender

Haven't I commanded you: be strong and courageous? Do not be afraid or discouraged, for the LORD your God is with you wherever you go." - Joshua 1:9 CSB

This verse is one that I always come back to whenever I'm feeling weak, discouraged, or afraid. After the death of Moses, God called Joshua, Moses' assistant, to lead the Israelites across the Jordan River and take possession of the Promised Land. God commanded Joshua to be strong and courageous as He guided and prepared him for the work he must do. It wasn't merely a suggestion to be strong and courageous but a command God gave him. This shows Joshua's weakness in that even as a great leader, he, too, needed encouragement.

Joshua didn't have the boldness or courage from his own strength but through God Himself. This is why God makes it a point to say, "Do not be afraid or discouraged, for the LORD your God is with you wherever you go." Joshua needed not to be afraid, not because of his own strength, but because God would be with him. Joshua's success was entirely dependent on God's presence with him.

We can relate this to our own lives when we fear stepping out in faith and leaning into the unknown. We face much uncertainty throughout our lives, and it can feel scary to trust that we are making the right decisions. This verse reminds us to be strong and courageous even when afraid because God is with us wherever we go. God encourages us to have faith and confidence even amidst hardships. God guides us every step of the way when we walk with Him, and we can rest knowing He will never leave or abandon us. The victory is promised when we press on seeking to do God's will.

Part of being strong is trusting in the Lord as our true source of strength. His power is perfected in our weakness (2 Corinthians 12:9). Joshua was weak and didn't know how to face the challenges ahead, but he stepped out in faith and trusted that God would lead, guide, and give him the strength he needed. God promises to provide us with that same strength. He knows what you are going through and what you need. He knows your battles and the decisions you need to make. Joshua 1:9 commands us to be strong and courageous because God is with us through it all.

Heartbreak is painful, and sometimes, we have to make hard decisions to let go. The future can seem uncertain and scary, but God promises to be with you and strengthen you. When we know what God is calling us to do, we can rest knowing He will get us through it, just like He did for Joshua. Going through a loss or breakup can make us fearful of letting go, but God commands us to be strong. When God told me to leave the toxic relationship I was in and to write a book about it, I was afraid to share my story for fear of what people would say or think, including my ex. Whenever I started to doubt, God reminded me of Joshua 1:9. This verse kept me going and helped push me forward because I knew if God called me to it, He would get me through it.

REFLECT/JOURNAL

What area in your life are you feeling discouraged and needing encouragement? Repeat this verse out loud to yourself, imagining God saying it to you. Where do you need God's strength? Ask God to send you encouragement today. Keep your eyes open for Him to speak to you today.

PRAYER

Dear Heavenly Father, thank You for always being faithful, even when I am afraid. Please give me the courage and strength I need to push forward in what You are calling me to do. Help me to trust

You when I feel discouraged and uncertain about the future. Thank You for always being with me wherever I go. Please continue to guide me and strengthen me like You did for Joshua. In Jesus' name, Amen.

Day 9: It's Not Forever

The God of all grace, who called you to his eternal glory in Christ, will himself restore, establish, strengthen, and support you after you have suffered a little while. - 1 Peter 5:10 CSB

After I got out of the toxic relationship I was in that was meant to destroy me, it was hard to trust that God had a plan. It's hard to believe there's an end to the suffering when you're in the middle of it. The suffering of these present times can make you wonder how you will ever heal or love again. Though it might seem impossible to recover, God has a plan of restoration for your life. I can confidently say that because if He did it for me, He can do it for you.

Peter makes it a point to say that God Himself will restore, establish, and strengthen us. Nowhere in this verse or the Bible does it say we are supposed to pick up all the broken pieces and put them together ourselves. God doesn't want us to rely on our own strength but, instead, to rely on Him to strengthen and restore us. We cannot face suffering and danger in our own strength. Sometimes, God will allow the suffering to teach us to be fully dependent and reliant on Him. I can testify this is true from personal experience.

God uses our suffering to shape and mold us. Just like a potter who shapes and molds clay as he pleases, God also shapes and molds us into the person He wants us to become. He strengthens our character through our trials, tribulations, and obstacles. Just like gold that is purified and refined only through the fire, God uses our suffering and trials to purify and refine our character. The purpose of the refining process is to remove any impurities so that it will come out as pure as possible. God does the same with our suffering to clean out the impurities in our lives. He puts us under the fire of affliction to cleanse us and make us more like Him.

To give you some hope and comfort, God restored everything I lost from my breakup. God restored things in my life that were broken long before I was even in my relationship. Following the breakup, God led me to a place of isolation from my old life and friends. Initially, I felt lost and alone. However, this period of solitude turned out to be the best thing God ever did for me. It was during this time that I learned how to hear God's voice and depend solely on Him for comfort. In the past, I had always relied on others to help and comfort me in my suffering. But now, God was no longer a last resort but my first and only option.

Through my pain and suffering, God taught me how to lean

on Him, and from there, I truly started walking with the Lord. If it weren't for that painful time in my life, I would have never grown my relationship with the Lord, and you wouldn't be reading this devotional right now. My suffering is what birthed my purpose. God restored, established, and strengthened me after I suffered a little while, and God will do the same for you.

REFLECT/JOURNAL

What emotions are you feeling right now? How can you bring them before God? In what ways has your suffering brought you closer to God? Write a letter to God telling Him your pain and how you need Him to comfort you. Write what you think He would say back to you. This can be very healing, as I've done this many times before. It brought me so much comfort that I read them back to myself whenever I needed encouragement.

PRAYER

Dear Heavenly Father, You are worthy of my praise no matter the suffering I am going through. I know You are still faithful, and I trust that You will use this suffering to purify and cleanse me of any impurities. Shape and mold me as You please so I can become who You intended me to be. Lord, teach me to fully rely and depend on You for strength and comfort. In Jesus' name, Amen.

Day 10: Overcoming Fear

I sought the Lord, and he answered me and rescued me from all my fears. - Psalm 34:4 CSB

When we are in a season of pain and suffering, it's tempting to want to reach for anything that takes the pain away, such as things like drugs or alcohol. There was a point in my life where that used to be me. I didn't think I could come to God when I messed up or was afraid because I was too ashamed or embarrassed to ask for God's help. Sometimes, I thought I was too far gone from God wanting to help me. But that's where I had it all wrong. It's very much the opposite. This verse gives us an example of God's character when David cried out to Him in fear; God answered and rescued him.

Fear can have a grip on us that can leave us with crippling anxiety. We fear our enemies coming after us, fear of the unknown, fear of never getting out of debt, fear of not being able to pay the bills, fear of never getting married, fear of being alone, fear of never being successful, fear of a health diagnosis, fear of leaving an unhealthy relationship, the list goes on. Psalm 34:4

shows us that David was experiencing fear before he sought the Lord for help because his enemies were coming after him. Our fears can make us anxious, but this verse reminds us that God hears our prayers and rescues us from all our fears.

Notice how this verse doesn't say, "he answered me and rescued me from *some* of my fears." It says, "he answered me and rescued me from *all* my fears." That is powerful! God wants to deliver us from *all* of our fears. God used to be my last resort when I was afraid because I didn't think He would show up until He did. When I was in my toxic relationship, I was living in constant anxiety and fear. One night, I wanted to leave for good, and I cried out to God, begging Him to help me. I didn't expect much to happen until God showed up and got me out literally the next day. He gave me the supernatural strength to finally leave that relationship for good, and I never looked back.

The biggest fear I had was when I was in a legal battle with my ex and was afraid of all the lies he would tell about me that weren't true, but God kept reminding me that He was in control and I didn't need to be. Whenever I sought the Lord for comfort, He showed up and reminded me I didn't need to be afraid. I've learned to put my complete trust in the Lord and trust that He will handle it. I started to fear less and trust more. It's not because I never faced trials again; it's because I went to God first every time I was afraid instead of last. I am grateful for all the trials I faced because they taught me how to depend entirely on God for

His help. He showed up every time I called out to Him.

God will meet you right where you are in your pain or fears. He is our Heavenly Father and doesn't like when we suffer. God hurts when we hurt. He is compassionate and loves us unconditionally. When you truly understand God's character, you will realize you can come to Him for anything and everything. You don't need to be embarrassed or ashamed when you are fearful.

You aren't meant to carry that burden on your own shoulders. Give it to God and ask Him to deliver you from your fears. Seeking out worldly things to comfort you might relieve the pain temporarily, but it will always leave you feeling empty. Let Psalm 34:4 encourage you to seek the Lord in times of trouble and fear, for He will answer and rescue you from all your fears.

REFLECT/JOURNAL

Fear never comes from God but from the enemy to discourage you. What current fears are you facing? Where does this fear come from? How have you sought the Lord to help deliver you from those fears? Tell God your fears and ask Him to deliver you from them and comfort you in the areas you need.

PRAYER

Dear Heavenly Father, I seek You with all my heart, mind, and soul. Help me strengthen my prayer life and understand Your character more. I want to know You deeper. Comfort me in my pain, Lord, and deliver me from all my fears. Thank You, Lord, that I can come to You anytime about anything, and You will listen. I will expectantly wait for You to answer. In Jesus' name, Amen.

Day 11: God's Purpose in Our Pain

But he said to me, "My grace is sufficient for you, for my power is perfected in weakness." - 2 Corinthians 12:9 CSB

Paul was writing to the Christians in Corinth about having a thorn in his flesh as a messenger of Satan to torment him so that he wouldn't exalt himself in his boasting about the revelations from the Lord. Paul prayed to the Lord about removing this thorn three times. God responded with, "My grace is sufficient for you, for my power is perfected in weakness." Instead of removing the thorn from Paul's life, God strengthened Paul through it so He could show His strength through Paul's weakness. I'm sure this is not the response Paul wanted to hear. I'm sure that's not the kind of response any of us would like to hear from God when we are hurting.

When we are in pain, we often seek a quick resolution. We wish God would alleviate our suffering so we don't have to endure it. The fact that Paul pleaded to God three times about this shows us that God didn't deliver him the first two times he prayed about it. Paul's initial response to this thorn in his flesh was to ask God to take away the suffering. When nothing changed after the third time he prayed for God to intervene, he realized there must be a reason why God was allowing it and not taking it away.

God doesn't delight in our suffering; He empathizes with our pain. This verse serves as a powerful reminder that even in our most trying times, God's grace is more than enough to carry us through. God might not remove the pain, but He promises to guide us through it. He could have easily taken away the thorn, but instead, He chose to strengthen Paul so he could endure it. God's intention was to demonstrate His strength even when Paul felt weak. Paul had even more reason to boast about his weaknesses because Christ's power was revealed through them. As Paul said, "For when I am weak, then I am strong" (2 Corinthians 12:10). This is a testament to the transformative power of God's grace and the strength we can find in our faith.

Through our suffering, God wants to demonstrate His strength to us. He doesn't take away the pain because there's something for us to learn. He wants to show us His strength through our weaknesses. However, this revelation can only come when we acknowledge our own limitations and our need for God's help. God's power won't be fully revealed if we think we can handle it on our own. We must first accept that we need

God to help us, and trust in His plan even when it's difficult to understand.

There's a purpose in the pain we face in life. When we go through things that seem unbearable, God steps in to show us that His grace is sufficient. It's in these moments of our deepest struggles that we truly get to see the power of God's grace, because we know there was no other way we would have gotten through it on our own. God knew the pain would be intense, but He also knew the transformative power it held. Your pain, as difficult as it may be, is preparing you for your purpose, shaping your character, and strengthening your faith.

I can speak from personal experience when I saw God's power through my suffering. When I thought I would never be able to get back up again, God showed up. I felt hopeless, defeated, and alone. I didn't even have the energy to pray because that's how hopeless I felt. But God knew I was in the perfect position to receive His healing power. He didn't take away the pain, but He strengthened me through it and made me stronger. It's hard to find hope in anything when we're in a place of brokenness, but that's when we truly see God's power work in our lives. His power is perfected in our weakness.

REFLECT/JOURNAL

What thorn have you been asking God to take

away? Instead of asking God to remove it, ask Him what lessons He might be trying to teach you through it. Take the time to write a letter to God, asking Him to give you strength and guidance through the pain. Don't hold back - express your genuine emotions and tell Him where you're hurting. Remember that God wants to help you on your journey and connect with you in your pain. Allow Him to minister to you while you write.

PRAYER

Dear Heavenly Father, thank You for Your healing power and grace, which are sufficient when I feel weak and broken. Help me to lean on You for strength to get me through this heartbreak. I can't do this on my own, Lord, so I need You to step in and lift me up. Please get me through this and show me Your glory. In Jesus' name, Amen.

Day 12: God Is the Provider

And my God will supply all your needs according to his riches in glory in Christ Jesus.
- Philippians 4:19 CSB

In Philippians 4:19, Paul promises the Philippians that God will supply all their needs according to His riches in glory in Christ Jesus. What exactly does this mean? Because that is a pretty big promise for the mere fact that God's riches are unlimited. The Philippians helped Paul with his clothing and food needs and some out of their own deep poverty. Paul was encouraging them that they wouldn't lack out of their giving because God would supply all of their needs. This is a promise that still stands for us today.

This one verse has gotten me through so many hardships regarding my finances. God's Word has proven time and time again that this is a promise. Now, this verse doesn't mean God will supply us with anything we want and make us rich, but it does mean that God knows what we need and will meet all of them so we will not lack the necessities in our everyday lives.

Once I understood this, it took so much pressure off of me that I didn't need to control how my needs would be met and that I could fully trust God to supply everything I needed.

This verse isn't just for our physical needs like finances but also for our spiritual needs such as wisdom, knowledge, comfort, love, encouragement, peace, joy, and anything else - the Lord has all we need. His resources are unlimited and infinite. All we must do is trust that He will provide everything we need. I have so many testimonies of how God paid my bills when I was worried about how I would come up with the money.

Every single time, God showed up and provided a way when there seemed to be no way. When God called me to move to a different state to pursue full-time ministry, I moved on faith with only $5,000 in my checking account. I didn't have a job lined up or know how I would afford to get my own apartment, much less pay my bills with no income coming in. Every month, I worried about how I would be able to pay a bill or even take my dog to the vet or buy him dog food, and every single time, God surprised me. He sustained me with His daily bread every single day, never missing a meal. I could write a whole book on testimonies like this.

Being in full-time ministry means relying on God for your finances every day. Unlike a typical job, you don't get a paycheck every two weeks or an hourly rate. Your money comes from voluntary donations from people sowing into the ministry. You have no control over how or when that happens. There would be times when I needed to pay a bill and would be on my knees asking God to provide, and within minutes, I would receive a donation from someone I didn't even know who found me on YouTube. I could write a whole book on all the times God did something like this for me. All it took was my faith and obedience.

Sometimes, God will allow us to have needs that need to be met so that we can seek Him more in prayer. He loves to show up in impossible ways that leave us speechless. He does this so He can get the glory and that we know it was only by Him and Him alone that our needs were met. I can also testify to this when I had the strength to move on after my breakup when I know without a shadow of doubt it was only because of God. God will supply all of your needs, and this is a promise. He already met the most significant need of all when He died on the cross for our sins, so what makes you think He won't meet your other basic needs?

REFLECT/JOURNAL

What needs are you currently needing God to meet? Write in detail about those needs and be specific. For example, if you need a financial need to be met, how much and for what? When we are specific with our prayers, it shows God that we have a specific need for a specific purpose. It shows our bold faith that we expect Him to answer regarding this need. Trust me, nothing is too big for God. Take the limits off of Him, and ask boldly what you need. After writing out your needs, pray over them and present your requests to Him. We don't go to a restaurant and say to the waitress, "Bring me food." No. We look at the menu and tell her exactly what we want and how we want it - "A burger cooked medium well with no tomatoes and a side of fries." Praying to God should be the same way.

PRAYER

Dear Heavenly Father, thank You for your unlimited resources that satisfy my every need. I trust that You will supply every need I have at the perfect time. You know what I am struggling with, and I pray that You help me depend on You to provide for me instead of putting my trust in anything else. You are the only security I need to rely on. You are the source of every need and my sole provider. In Jesus' name, Amen.

Day 13: Leave It to God

Friends, do not avenge yourselves; instead, leave room for God's wrath, because it is written, Vengeance belongs to me; I will repay, says the Lord. - Romans 12:19 CSB

After any breakup, it can be easy to fall into bitterness and unforgiveness. We play out scenarios trying to make ourselves feel better by justifying where the other person hurt us or did us wrong. This is a common defense mechanism to protect our emotions and help us get over someone by resenting them. I can be the first to admit that is how I used to approach all my breakups in the past. It was easier that way, and it helped mask the pain I was feeling. Being angry at them was more manageable than missing them and admitting I was hurt. I would think of ways to get back at them so they would miss me and regret the breakup. But that approach always seemed to do more harm than good, leaving me even more sad when it didn't work.

Romans 12:19 tells us that vengeance belongs to God, not to us. He knows what you went through and what happened in your relationship and will repay accordingly. It is not up to us to get revenge. God wants us to be free and give it to Him. When my ex cheated on me multiple times and caused me pain, all I wanted was for him to feel the same pain he put me through. I wanted God to punish him and make him hurt how he hurt me. I was bitter and angry. But all it did was fill me with hatred and unforgiveness and hardened my heart. It didn't make me feel better about the situation; it only made me feel worse.

The Bible says not to repay evil for evil (Romans 12:17) but to bless those who curse us (Romans 12:14). How we show up when people hurt us truly exposes what's in our hearts and where we put our trust. If we truly trust God, we will leave vengeance up to God and have no part in it, knowing He will take care of it. When we leave the situation up to God, it sets us free from worrying about it.

God saw all and will take care of it as He sees fit. It is His responsibility to take avenge in the way He chooses to. But when we try to take things into our own hands, it often leads to destruction and does more damage to us than to them. Most of the time, you will regret even doing what you did because when you are emotional, you are irrational. God is more than able to take care of the people who wrong us. He doesn't need our help to do it; He is more than capable of taking care of it on His own. Let God deal with your prosecutors. God is your defender, and you can trust that He has your back. Our hearts must stay pure so God sees how we act when our flesh wants revenge.

We may never get to see or witness how God chooses to avenge the ones who hurt us, but we must trust and believe He will take care of it in His own way. If we truly trust that God will take care of it, we let go of wanting to get even with the people who hurt us. We have nothing to worry about, knowing that God uses everything for our good, even from the ones who hurt us.

We cannot let our emotions overrule our character. Proverbs 16:32 says, "Patience is better than power, and controlling one's emotions, than capturing a city." This verse tells us that controlling our emotions is better than conquering a city. That is powerful! Not only is it godly to control our emotions, but it also shows God that we have complete trust in Him to handle it. The battle is not yours. It belongs to the Lord. Let Him fight for you. We must let go, leave the vengeance up to God, and trust that He will handle it.

REFLECT/JOURNAL

Do you believe that God is capable of avenging you from your situation? Are there any doubts you have about this verse? Do you feel the urge to get even with your ex or hurt them back? If so, it shows that you don't believe in what Paul says here. What emotions are you struggling with? Do you find it challenging to control your emotions or have trouble believing that God will take care of your situation?

PRAYER

Dear Heavenly Father, I am sorry for the times I've wanted revenge on the people who have hurt me. I know that You are the One in control and that vengeance belongs to You. Help me rest, knowing You are the One who fights for me. I know this battle is not mine to fight but Yours. I surrender my need for control to want to pay back the ones who hurt me, and I give it to You instead. Lord, please give me the mercy to handle my emotions with grace and help me to forgive the ones who hurt me. I put all my trust in You. In Jesus' name, Amen.

Day 14: Comfort in God's Presence

Even when I go through the darkest valley, I fear no danger, for you are with me; your rod and your staff - they comfort me. - Psalm 23:4 CSB

Psalm 23 is one of the most well-known Psalms that have comforted people in the darkest times. This verse gives us a powerful metaphor to describe these dark times as a valley. This verse illustrates that we will face a dark valley of our own from trials and suffering at some point in our lives, but when we do, we should fear not, knowing God is by our side through it. "I fear no danger" shows us that we can be confident in God's protection from evil. This verse should give you so much peace that God will provide calmness and comfort when you feel fearful or overwhelmed.

When I was healing from my breakup, I felt so alone and defeated. Nothing seemed to make me feel better except talking to God about it. I kept asking Him to comfort me and let me know He was with me through the pain. When I came across this verse, it gave me so much comfort because I just knew God was speaking to me. I wrote this verse down everywhere, read it every day, and memorized it so whenever I felt alone, I would repeat it out loud. It instantly brought me comfort and made me feel better.

The rod and staff David refers to in this Psalm are instruments a shepherd used. The rod was a tool to protect the flock from predators, and the staff guided and directed the sheep. These two instruments represent God's guidance and protection. Knowing that God is always looking out for us and that we are under His care at all times, even through our darkest or lowest times, should bring us much comfort and peace. God is our shepherd and will protect and guide us.

Going through a breakup is painful, and it hurts. When we are suffering, we wish to fast forward and heal. But did you know there's a purpose why God doesn't take the pain away? He teaches us through the pain. When we are broken, we have the heart posture to be vulnerable. It throws pride and ego out the window. Being in a broken and vulnerable state is the perfect place where God's voice can be heard. I know this was true for me. I felt God's presence the most when I was at my lowest because I was still enough to hear His voice.

God is close to the brokenhearted. When we cry out to Him, He hears us and wants to comfort us. But we have to let Him comfort us. We have to sit there long enough for Him to show up. If we never sit long enough to give Him the time to show up, we won't be able to hear Him. I know it's easy to want to distract yourself to keep yourself busy, but being busy could be the very thing that is blocking you from feeling God's presence. Allow God to comfort you by asking Him to. He wants to hear from you. Just know that He is still working on your behalf even when you can't see or feel Him.

REFLECT/JOURNAL

What valley are you going through right now? Close your eyes and picture Jesus standing beside you, wanting to talk to you. He is right there ready for you to invite Him in. Tell Him what you are afraid of and be vulnerable. Write down what you feel Him saying to you. Give God enough time to answer you. Ask Him to comfort you and speak to you. Write this verse down, and memorize and meditate on it.

PRAYER

Dear Heavenly Father, thank You for Your protection and guidance. Thank You for being my Shepherd in Whom I trust. I pray You keep me out of harm's way and protect me from any danger that crosses my path. Lord, I pray You comfort me through the dark valley I am walking through. Remind me You are with me even when I feel alone. In Jesus' name, Amen.

Day 15: Trusting God in the Unknown

Trust in the LORD with all your heart, and do not lean on your own understanding. In all your ways acknowledge him, and he will make straight your paths. - Proverbs 3:5-6 ESV

When we are suffering, we want it to make sense so we can understand. We question everything and overthink, playing out different scenarios of why it is the way it is. Trust me, I know, because I am the biggest overthinker in the world. I want everything to make sense. I must ensure all the pieces fit together to be at peace. I hate when things don't make sense. However, overthinking is a tactic of the enemy because it keeps us distracted from praying and putting our focus on God.

God's wisdom is incomprehensible and profound. We aren't meant to understand the ways of God because it wouldn't make sense to us, and it's not supposed to. God says we are to trust Him with all our heart and lean not on our own understanding. He knows our ways and understanding are limited, and we don't know what's best for us like we think we do; only God does. God knows what we need more than we do, even if it doesn't make sense to us. His wisdom and knowledge surpass all understanding beyond our human comprehension.

God says we are to acknowledge Him in all our ways, and He will make our paths straight. That is a promise we can stand on, and I can speak from my own experiences of how true that is. So many times in my life, things didn't make sense when I was going through certain situations or losing people. I was so confused and hurt, not understanding its reason or purpose. Looking back, I can see how God protected me from things He knew that I didn't at the time. The ways of God are so above our heads, and when something happens in our lives that we don't understand, we have to trust that God has a purpose for it. God is very intentional about the way things unfold in our lives.

When it comes to heartbreak specifically, our emotions can blind us and cause us to think irrationally. We can't rely on our feelings because they aren't based on facts. We need to hold the Word of God above our emotions. God knows what is best for us, so when He takes things away, it's either to protect us or save us. God sees the bigger picture, and you can trust Him to put you on the right path. The reassurance in knowing that we can surrender all control to a sovereign God is deeply comforting. It takes the pressure off of us when we truly put our trust in Him to guide us.

If you truly trust God, you will give up your making sense of things and give it all to Him. It's a promise that He will make your paths straight if you acknowledge Him in all your ways. I know you want things to make sense so you can feel better going through this pain, but God's wisdom doesn't even compare to ours. Believe and trust in the One who has our best interests at heart. He has it all calculated down to the very second of what will happen in your life. God knows every intricate detail of your life, including the number of hairs on your head (Luke 12:7).

When I went through my breakup, I didn't understand the purpose of why God would allow me to suffer so much with someone I wasn't supposed to be with. I can now see how God used it to propel me into my purpose to help others. Before that relationship, I had no purpose. When I got out of that relationship, God revealed to me my life's mission and purpose. If you fully put your trust in Him, He will make your paths straight and do more than you ever thought was possible. This heartbreak may feel like a setback, but it could very much be the setup God will use to propel you into your destiny. Setbacks are setups in disguise.

REFLECT/JOURNAL

Think of a time in the past when you put your trust in God to get you through a situation. Write about those times and reflect on how it turned out. Did it all work out in the end? Sometimes, things don't work out in our favor at the moment, but usually, it ends up working out for the best. How can you apply this to your current situation? Ask God to help you let go and fully surrender it all to Him. Remembering God's past faithfulness is key to future victories.

PRAYER

Dear Heavenly Father, thank You for Your infinite wisdom that is always protecting and guiding me. Please help me to trust You with all my heart even when I don't understand. I am grateful that Your thoughts are greater than my thoughts, and Your ways are higher than my ways. Thank You for making my paths straight. I can trust and rest, knowing my life is in Your hands. In Jesus' name, Amen.

Day 16: Give It to God

Cast your burden on the Lord, and he will sustain you; he will never allow the righteous to be shaken. - Psalm 55:22 CSB

In this verse, David is deeply distressed after being betrayed by one of his best friends. His best friend now became an enemy, and David was overwhelmed with grief. On top of this betrayal, he had multiple threats and attacks from his enemies, who were after him from every angle. Even David knew his burden was one that God could bear and handle. Sometimes, God gives us burdens He knows are too much for us, so He can see what we do with them. Will we hold on to it and let it weigh us down, or will we cast it onto the Lord?

When we cast our burdens on the Lord, He promises to sustain us through it. He doesn't take away the suffering experience, but He makes it more bearable so we can have the strength to endure it. We are not meant to carry our burdens on our own. God knows we aren't strong enough to hold the weight of all our problems. I have tried to carry the pain and hurt in my life on my own for many years before I knew anything about the Bible. Carrying the heaviness of my burdens left me feeling exhausted, drained, and burnt out. I was filled with so much anxiety daily because the pain was just overwhelming.

The last breakup I went through, as I write this devotional, I chose to do things differently. I wanted to do it God's way this time because I was exhausted from trying it my way. Every day, I cast all the heaviness of my pain onto the Lord. I still can't explain the supernatural strength God gave me to walk away from that relationship and move on. It used to take me years to get over someone I had dated for a long time because of how attached I was. After my last breakup, I thought I would be healing for a decade with how much pain it caused me. I felt that would be my breaking point and that I would be destroyed forever. But I cried out to God one night to help me because I wanted out of this toxic relationship cycle for good. I wanted to be healed for real this time so that I would never accept toxic behavior again.

What would have usually taken me years to heal from something like this by myself took only seven months with God. God helped me hold my head up even when I was in pain. Even when hurting, I felt an unexplainable peace because I knew God was with me. The healing process didn't seem long because I focused on God, not my ex. God truly sustained me and refreshed my spirit. When we fix our eyes on Jesus instead of our pain, He will supernaturally give us the strength to bear it.

God's grace will have you come out of the fire, not even smelling like smoke. When God restores you, you won't look anything like what you've been through. I can confidently say that because I don't look or act like anything I've been through.

I am an overthinker by nature and tend to be a control freak. Being in control of everything eliminated any chance of being let down and disappointed. When I started learning about the Bible and realized I could cast my burdens on the Lord, that felt like such a foreign concept. I've always been the strong friend where everyone comes to me, but I've never been one to put my burdens on someone else. At first, my pride got in the way of giving my problems to God. I didn't know how to give someone else my burdens without feeling awkward or bad about it.

I kept my problems to myself because I didn't want to burden anyone. I didn't know how to talk to God about my problems. When I went through my severe last breakup, I gave it a try because I was desperate for relief. I cast everything onto God and gave Him all my burdens and emotions. I was honest with God and told Him how hurt and frustrated I was. It was unexplainable how much better I felt afterward and the peace that came over me. It instantly felt like the weight was lifted from my shoulders. Let this devotional encourage you today to cast your burdens onto the Father so He can sustain you through it.

REFLECT/JOURNAL

Are you trying to carry the weight of your burdens on your own, or are you casting it onto the Lord? Be honest and tell God your burdens so He can take them off your shoulders. Tell Him your emotions and your frustrations, and let them out. I'm sure you will feel a huge weight come off of you. Journaling is one of the best ways to do this.

PRAYER

Dear Heavenly Father, thank You for allowing me to come to You with my burdens. Thank You for carrying the weight when I can't. Please help me to go to You when I feel overwhelmed with grief. Lord, I acknowledge that I cannot carry these burdens on my own. I know that no matter what I am up against, Your Word promises to sustain me. Remind me that I can lay it all on You, God. In Jesus' name, Amen.

Day 17: God Is the Healer

He heals the brokenhearted and binds up their wounds. - Psalm 147:3 NIV

No matter the depth of your heartbreak, God can repair your wounds. No matter how painful or deep the wound, God can heal you. This verse is a promise we can stand on that God is our healer. He is the "Great Physician" and better than any doctor out there. His healing power is supernatural and divine. As a child of God, we have access to the healing power of our Father. God wants to take you from a place of suffering to a place of rest.

You may feel shattered and broken right now, but God promises to put it back together and restore your heart. He doesn't just promise to put a bandaid over it but to heal you from the inside out and mend your heart back together. The Hebrew word for "heals" in Psalm 147:3 is *Rapha*, which doesn't just mean returning to normal health but fully restoring to perfect healing. In other words, it means to mend by stitching or to make whole. God wants to stitch your broken heart and restore it to perfect wholeness.

God has an excellent track record for healing broken hearts. He has had the worst patients and yet has never lost one. God doesn't just give you access to medicine; He is the medicine. We have the best medicine at our fingertips, ready to be used. God gives us His Word and His Holy Spirit power as our medicine. All we need to do is call on Him for help and ask Him to heal us. Just as physical wounds can heal, internal wounds can also heal by the power and grace of God. He knows the true severity of your broken heart and can bring it back to restoration better than it was before.

After my painful breakup, my heart felt like it was shattered into a million pieces. It all happened so quickly and left me feeling broken and confused. I couldn't make it make sense, which was the most difficult part to accept. Accepting things when you understand is easy, but accepting things when you don't understand is much more painful and challenging. I didn't think anything could heal how I felt on the inside. The road to recovery felt forever away. I didn't want to go through the healing process and face my emotions and wounds. I wanted a quick fix and to wake up from the nightmare I felt like I was in. God taught me significant lessons and gave me wisdom from that breakup that could never be bought. One thing I've learned is that there's pain in the recovery process, and it's necessary for healing.

Through my healing journey, I clung to God more than I ever thought was possible. I heard Him speak to me in ways I have never experienced before. The love I felt from Him overwhelmed me in the best way. I became addicted to getting in His presence. Where I once had a gaping hole in my heart from someone who broke it, God filled it and restored it with His unconditional love. Had I not been at my lowest place of desperation, I would have never discovered what it truly meant to be loved. God taught me what it felt like to be truly loved and safe. How could I have ever known what "true love" was if I had not first discovered God's love for me?

My perception of love completely changed, and God revealed to me why I had accepted breadcrumbs my whole life. When we don't know what it's like to be truly loved by God, we won't be able to recognize what true love is with another human. Therefore, we can confuse relationships as love when, in actuality, it's nowhere close. Our relationship with our Heavenly Father determines what kind of relationships we accept and entertain. Sometimes, God will allow your heart to get broken to show you what love truly is. Our relationship with others can only be as deep as our relationship with God. We can't love or receive love properly if we don't even know what it's like to love or be loved by God first.

The love of God will always outweigh the love of man. God will restore and heal your heart better than the state it was in before the heartbreak you experienced. Nothing heals like the love of the Father. You might be at rock bottom, but God has you there for a reason, so you can know His true power when He heals you from a place you never thought you could get out of. Through this heartbreak, God is teaching you what it's like first to be loved by Him, so when the next person comes along, you can discern if God sent this person.

REFLECT/JOURNAL

Do you know what it's like to be truly loved by God? Can you look back on past relationships where you felt like it was true love only to find out it wasn't? How was your relationship with God then? Do you have difficulty receiving or believing God's love for you? Ask God what the purpose of your broken heart is, and allow Him space to answer you. Write down what you feel He would say to you.

PRAYER

Dear Heavenly Father, thank You for Your promise to heal my broken heart and bind up my wounds. My heart is hurting, and I need Your healing power to heal and restore me. May I put all my trust in You to put me back together again and make me whole. Teach me what it's like to be loved by You so I can understand and recognize what true love is. Allow my relationships to be an extension of Your love. Teach me the lessons in my pain and help me to use them for Your glory. Thank You, Father, for Your unfailing love. In Jesus' name, Amen.

Day 18: God Will Restore You

Then he will restore your fortunes, have compassion on you, and gather you again from all the peoples where the LORD your God has scattered you. - Deuteronomy 30:3 CSB

One of the hardest things to come to terms with after my breakup was how much time I felt I lost while being in the wrong relationship – one that hurt and destroyed me. The relationship was not only physically damaging but mentally, emotionally, and financially as well. I was worried I would never return to who I was before that relationship. I was mad at myself for staying longer than I should have and for how many years of my life felt wasted. I carried so much shame and resentment until I came across this verse a few months after my breakup. This verse encouraged me because I felt God speaking right into my situation.

Going through a breakup can feel like someone just pulled a rug from underneath you, leaving you breathless on the floor.

You sit in disbelief, wondering how it even got to this point and if you will ever feel whole again. Let this verse encourage you that God is a restorer and puts broken pieces back together. He will restore everything you thought you lost, including the years you wasted in the wrong relationship. Nothing is a waste when God gets ahold of it. God will restore your heart, mind, time, finances, joy, and anything else that relationship took from you. God knows what you lost, and He will gather you from where you were scattered and restore your fortunes. Regardless of what you've lost, you can stand on what the Word of God says – He won't leave you scattered.

After my breakup, I had a lot of negative thoughts that were conditioned from when I was little. Thoughts such as, "I'm *not good enough,*" "*No one will ever love me,*" "*See, everyone leaves me,*" "*Another failed relationship yet again,*" "*Is something wrong with me,*" "*I don't feel worthy of finding real love,*" "*I'm never chosen.*" Do these thoughts sound familiar? I realized I had a lot of reprogramming to do in my mind. I started diving into the Bible for hours daily and replacing my negative thought patterns with what the Word of God says. I wanted to completely change my mindset and become the woman God intended for me to be. For God to renew my mind, I knew I had to start by addressing the lies I believed about myself and replacing them with God's truth.

Deuteronomy 30:3 is one of the verses I wrote down when I

addressed the lie, "*I lost everything from that breakup, and I'll never get back the time I lost.*" I reminded myself that God's Word says He will restore my fortunes and have compassion for me. I kept meditating and repeating God's truth until I memorized it. I would do this every day for a few weeks until it became a regular part of my life. I would walk, saying in my head, "I can do all things through Christ who strengthens me," whenever I felt like I couldn't keep going. Doing this became my new way of living and became a habit. When you start replacing your negative thoughts with the Word of God, you give no foothold to the enemy to attack your mind.

God will gather all the broken pieces of your life, no matter where you have been scattered. He will restore everything you lost, including your time. No matter where you are, even if you feel stuck in the trenches, God will rescue you if you call out to Him. He doesn't keep a tally of your mistakes; His grace and mercy are enough to lift you back up. God's love and compassion, which are immeasurable and infinite, are beyond what we can understand. No amount of pain, grief, or trial can ever separate you from the love of your Heavenly Father.

REFLECT/JOURNAL

What do you feel you've lost from this breakup/relationship? What parts of yourself do you feel have been taken away? Do you believe God can restore them? Where do you need restoration from God?

PRAYER

Dear Heavenly Father, Your faithfulness never ceases to amaze me. Lord, I ask You to restore everything I lost as a result of that relationship. Please restore the years I lost and renew my spirit. Fill me with Your joy so that I can experience laughter and happiness again. I pray that You help me to renew my mind, and gather all the broken pieces of my life together again. In Jesus' name, Amen.

DAY 19: NO PRAYER IS OFF LIMITS

DO NOT BE ANXIOUS ABOUT ANYTHING, BUT IN EVERY SITUATION, BY PRAYER AND PETITION, WITH THANKSGIVING, PRESENT YOUR REQUESTS TO GOD. AND THE PEACE OF GOD, WHICH TRANSCENDS ALL UNDERSTANDING, WILL GUARD YOUR HEARTS AND YOUR MINDS IN CHRIST JESUS. - PHILIPPIANS 4:6-7 NIV

God's care extends to every little detail of our lives, providing a comforting reassurance. No prayer is ever too big or too small for God to care about. Even the seemingly insignificant prayer requests we might hesitate to bring to God's attention are not. If God cares to feed the sparrows and dress the lilies, how much more does He care about your broken heart? I used to think I could only come to God with significant prayer requests, such as healing a family member in the hospital or having a safe flight on an airplane. That was the extent of my prayer life before I got saved and deepened my relationship with God more intimately.

As I write this book, my prayer life has undergone a complete transformation. I now engage in conversations with God about everything, including asking Him how to spend my money or what opportunities I should say yes or no to. This shift in my prayer life has brought me closer to God, making me realize that He cares about the things I care about. God is not just our Father in Heaven, but also our friend. We can talk to Him like we talk to our friends. Our friends care about the little details of our lives, so why wouldn't God? Just as we seek our friends' advice on what to wear for an event or what to order at a restaurant, we can talk to God about the things that matter to us. God cares about what we care about.

God tells us in this verse not to be anxious about anything; it is a command, not a request or an option. Instead, He tells us to pray about everything. Nothing is off-limits that we can't pray about or that God doesn't care about. James 4:2 tells us that we have not because we ask not. Many of our prayers go unanswered because we do not ask God. We can come to God with our requests and make them known. If you need help with anything or a prayer you need answered, you can ask God. This verse is an invitation to come to Him about anything and everything under the sun.

Many don't come to God with prayer requests because they think, "Well, isn't He God? Doesn't He already know about my situation and what I need?" Yes, of course, He knows everything you are going through. Still, He will often wait for our participation through prayer before granting our requests. If we don't pray or come to God about the things we need, how would we know it was God who answered? God loves when we go to Him about what we need because it is an opportunity for Him to show us His glory when our prayers are answered. God already knows what you need before you ask Him. We don't pray to let God know what we need; we pray to partner up with God so He can move on our behalf. While we actively wait, He actively works.

God knows the heartbreak you are going through. He knows every detail of it and every thought you have. God knows what you are thinking from when you wake up to when you go to bed. He knows what you need and what you want. He knows when you are anxious and when you are upset. Let this verse remind you to call on God when you feel overwhelmed and ask Him to still your mind.

When you find yourself overwhelmed with emotions, instead of dwelling on your feelings, you can turn to God for help. This practice can bring a profound sense of relief and peace. Every time I felt overwhelmed with emotions, I turned on worship music, closed my eyes, and prayed for God to calm me down and ease my anxiety. I have noticed that my anxiety dissipates almost instantly every time I call upon God for help, as opposed to attempting to manage it on my own. God is always available to step into your situation when you go to Him in prayer. You are never alone in this; with God's help, you can emerge victorious.

RELFECT/JOURNAL

Have you been avoiding prayer because you're not sure what to say or how to say it? Is there something that you need God to do for you but haven't asked Him yet? Remember that you don't need to have all the right words or perfect phrasing. God wants to hear from you, just as you are. Let this be the opportunity to get deep and vulnerable with God about the things that have been weighing on you. You might be surprised at the peace and clarity that can come from an honest conversation with Him.

PRAYER

Dear Heavenly Father, I am grateful for Your care and concern for every aspect of my life. I recognize that I cannot control everything, and I do not want to be overwhelmed by anxiety or negative emotions. Please help me calm my mind and turn to You whenever doubt, fear, or anxiety threaten to take over. I know that I can pray about anything, and I ask that You take control of all my worries and concerns. I trust You to guide me through this difficult time and fill my heart and mind with Your comfort and peace. In Jesus' name, Amen.

DAY 20: A FRESH START

"FORGET THE FORMER THINGS; DO NOT DWELL ON THE PAST. SEE, I AM DOING A NEW THING! NOW IT SPRINGS UP; DO YOU NOT PERCEIVE IT? I AM MAKING A WAY IN THE WILDERNESS AND STREAMS IN THE WASTELAND. - ISAIAH 43:18-19 NIV

When God closes one door, He opens another. When He tells us to put something down, it is because He has something better for us to pick up. We can't pick up the new thing if we are holding on to the old thing. In this verse, God is saying to forget the past so you can see the new thing He is getting ready to do in your life. You won't be able to perceive the new thing if you constantly focus on the past. God will never tell us to let go of something if He didn't intend to replace it with something better. He wants to give you a fresh start to something new, a start that is free from the burdens of the past, a start that brings relief and liberation.

Letting go of a relationship can feel like you are in a dry wilderness, but God promises to make a way with streams in the wasteland. God wants you to keep your eyes ahead, not behind. I know how easy it is to dwell on the past hurt from your relationship and play out scenario after scenario of how things could have been different. The enemy loves to keep us in this cycle of shame and guilt from our past so that we never see what God is doing in the present. As long as we keep our eyes on the past, we will never step into the blessings God has for us in the future. God doesn't just close doors by accident; He knows exactly what He's doing and has a purpose behind every open or closed door.

A constant theme in the Bible is to trust God even when we don't understand. God's ways are higher than our ways, and His thoughts are greater than our thoughts (Isaiah 55:8). I know how painful losing someone is, but the good news is that God has already worked everything out. If we truly trust God, we must allow Him to lead us to new places even if it doesn't make sense to us. This trust in His plan brings a sense of security and reassurance, knowing that He is always guiding us in the right direction.

To fully surrender to God means to take our hands off the situation so He can steer us in the right direction. We can't help Him steer by trying to control the situation, just like two people can't drive simultaneously. Only one person can control the steering wheel, and we must let go of control so God can sit in the driver's seat. If God's ways are better than our ways, we must trust that He has a better plan for us. God would never steer us in the wrong direction. Just like a shepherd guides and protects their sheep, God does the same for us; He is our shepherd.

God is always working, even when we can't see or feel it. What may seem like a loss now will turn into a gain in the future. Every time I went through a breakup, it felt excruciatingly painful because I found it hard to let go of people who were a significant part of my life. I spent so much time dwelling on the past that I never had time to focus on God. I let my emotions and feelings consume my time, which became obsessive and unhealthy. I would sit there playing out every scenario, reminiscing on memories, and thinking about how things could have been different.

When I put my focus on God instead of the past after my last breakup, He opened my eyes, and everything changed. I gave God the steering wheel and surrendered to where He was guiding me. I put my focus on the future instead of the past. I trusted that where God was taking me was better than where He found me. I have personally experienced the truth of Isaiah 43:18-19. The breakup that I thought would destroy me became a blessing in disguise. It helped me heal deep wounds from my past and brought me closer to Jesus. This healing process was not easy, but it was necessary for my growth and transformation.

Although I couldn't see it then, God was with me every step of the way. I kept pushing forward until I finally felt like I could breathe again. Following where God led me was such a blessing that I never wanted to look back. He opened doors I could have never imagined had I stayed stuck in the past. God doesn't force us into the new; He invites us. We have the choice to move forward with God or remain trapped in our past. "See, I am doing a new thing" is an invitation to perceive what He is currently doing in your life right now. Even in your pain, He still paves the way for the new.

REFLECT/JOURNAL

What new thing is the Lord doing in your life right now? How do you perceive God paving a new path for you? Are you willing to accept the invitation to step into the new, or are you struggling to let go of the past? What is holding you back from moving forward completely and why? Take a moment to reflect on these questions as you journal.

PRAYER

Dear Heavenly Father, I pray that You help me learn the lessons from my past without dwelling on them. Please show me the new things You are doing in my life right now. I also pray that You help me forgive myself and others for past mistakes so I don't live in shame or guilt. Instead, I want to walk towards the new things You have in store for me. I surrender my need for control and ask that You guide and steer me in the right direction. Thank You for being my shepherd Who guides me through the wilderness. In Jesus' name, Amen.

Day 21: The Bigger Picture

You intended to harm me, but God intended it for good to accomplish what is now being done, the saving of many lives. - Genesis 50:20 NIV

If I could choose one verse I resonate with the most, it would be this one. The toxic and abusive relationship I was in came to destroy my life. If it wasn't for God giving me the strength to leave, I can honestly say that it might have killed me. But because of how good God is, He turned it all around and used it for good, which is now helping many others through similar situations. I have inspired and helped thousands of people by sharing my testimony on social media and hundreds through my books and coaching sessions. God knew what He was doing when I went through that relationship.

When we encounter hardships in our lives, we might wonder why we have to endure them. However, we must remember that God plans to use these experiences to help others going through similar situations. Our struggles give us wisdom and insight that can help us be a guiding light to others who are struggling, too.

We may not always understand why we face difficult situations, but we can be confident that God has a purpose for everything. The harder the trials, the greater the purpose.

Even if we cannot see it now, we can believe that God has a plan for us. He can transform what we once thought was shattered into something beautiful. In Genesis 50:20, Joseph speaks this verse to his brothers to comfort them as he knew they felt guilty for selling him as a slave years prior. God had a plan for Joseph's suffering, even when he was put in prison.

If Joseph had not been sold as a slave, he would have never been put in prison, where he interpreted dreams. If Joseph had never interpreted dreams in prison, he would have never interpreted Pharaoh's dreams and become prime minister. If he had never become prime minister, he would not have been able to prepare for the famine, which ultimately saved his entire family from dying in Canaan. God used all the events in Joseph's life for his good. Even when humans plan evil against us and succeed, God can take it and use it for good to accomplish a greater purpose; it's all a setup.

Ultimately, our lives are in God's hands, ruling over any evil plan that man may have. Joseph trusted God's plan, allowing him to show his brothers love and compassion. Joseph was able to save his entire family's life all because, years prior, his brothers sold him as a slave. God set that up because He knew what was up ahead. Although they meant harm against him, God turned it around not only for good but also for the saving of many lives.

God can do the same for you, even in your heartbreak. God is aware of your struggles and knows what you are going through. Even though it may seem impossible to envision a better future, trust that God is working behind the scenes. If someone had told me a year ago that I would be writing books to help people heal through heartbreak, coaching others as a Christian relationship coach, creating videos on social media about God, and being in full-time ministry, I would have thought they were crazy.

I didn't know a toxic relationship would lead me into my purpose, but God did. God used what was meant to harm me as a setup and turned it around for my good, giving me purpose. We need to adopt a Joseph mindset when we face trials. Trust that God will turn your situation around for good because He is known to bring beauty out of ashes. You could be right in the middle of a setup.

REFLECT/JOURNAL

Are you putting your complete trust in God in your current situation? Do you have faith God will turn this into something good? Remember, adopting a Joseph-like mindset means trusting in God's plan, even when it's difficult. Take the time to write a prayer of forgiveness to the person who has hurt you, not because what they did was acceptable, but because you know God will bring good out of it. You don't need to physically give this to them, as it is meant to help you and not them. It is to help you release any bitterness and anger you may be holding onto. Having unforgiveness in your heart can block your blessings and hinder your growth. As for myself, I can say that I am grateful for my ex and the difficulties he put me through because it ultimately led me to Jesus and my life's purpose. My ex gave me the platform that I now use to inspire others. So, thank whoever hurt you because it will be the reason for your elevation and growth.

PRAYER

Dear Heavenly Father, I am grateful for Your presence in my life. I thank You in advance for turning the things that were meant to harm and destroy me around for my good. I pray that You will use every part of my situation to help others someday. Please give me the strength to have faith in Your bigger plan when I feel discouraged. Even when it feels painful and hurts, I know that You are still good. I trust You even when I cannot see all of what You are doing. In Jesus' name, Amen.

Day 22: More than Enough

Now to him who is able to do far more abundantly than all that we ask or think, according to the power at work within us. - Ephesians 3:20 ESV

Whatever you are seeking from God, He is more than capable of exceeding your expectations. He is not a God of mere sufficiency but of abundance. He is not a God of just enough, but more than enough. Whenever I ask God to surprise me beyond my imagination, I recite Ephesians 3:20, one of my favorite verses. In my first book, *Better Days After a Toxic Relationship*, I wrote from a place of brokenness, struggling and uncertain about how God would answer my prayers. Yet, it was through my act of obedience, writing my book in my broken state, that I found healing.

I firmly believe that God orchestrated the writing of my book during my weakest moments. It's fascinating how God often gives us divine assignments at our lowest. Perhaps it's because He knows that our most profound work can emerge from the crucible of adversity, just as musicians often produce their best music during trials. God knew that I would be writing that book during one of my most vulnerable times, making it relatable to the reader. If I had written that book when I was completely healed, it would have been a much different story and less relatable to the reader.

When I began writing my first book, I thought it would just be a simple e-book. Despite my lack of knowledge and uncertainty about where this would lead me, I continued to have faith in God and trusted the process. Every day, I prayed that God would use my book to touch the lives of people all over the world beyond what I could ever imagine. As I kept writing, I found myself having so much more to say than I had anticipated; God was guiding my words, and I couldn't stop typing. The length of my book grew to a point where it became a full-fledged book. God knew what it would be all along. Sometimes, God only shows us the first step to take so that we won't get overwhelmed if He were to show us the whole vision.

Months later, my book was published on Amazon and has now reached thousands of people in over 15 countries. Not only that, but it was the number-one new release on Amazon for two weeks in a row! It also inspired me to start a coaching business that helps women heal and recover from toxic and narcissistic relationships from a biblical standpoint. Next thing you know, my ministry was birthed. It's incredible to see how God can take our one small act of obedience and use it to propel us into our purpose and calling. It's a powerful reminder that one step of obedience can make all the difference.

You never know how God is setting things up for you, even at your rock bottom. The heartbreak you are facing now could be a setup for your purpose, a launching pad to your destiny. This was certainly the case for me. I could have never seen it coming, but God sure did. I never expected my life to be where it is now, but God did more than I ever could have imagined. Remember that God doesn't allow you to break down without a breakthrough. So, hold on just a little bit longer because your turn is coming. Get ready for God to do immeasurably more than you could ever ask, think, or imagine, and move in a way you have never experienced before.

REFLECT/JOURNAL

Have you been feeling a nudging from God to start something? If you're unsure, take a moment to ask Him what He wants you to do. What is one step of obedience you can take now? Remember, obeying His call can lead to a greater plan and purpose for your life.

PRAYER

Dear Heavenly Father, I am grateful for Your Word that renews my spirit. Lord, I trust that Your plans for me are good, but I pray that You will go beyond my expectations and do more than I could ever imagine. Please reveal to me the purpose behind the struggles I am facing, and help me to use these trials as a stepping stone towards fulfilling my destiny. Teach me the lessons You want me to learn, and show me how I can bring glory to Your name through this experience. In Jesus' name, Amen.

DAY 23: WAITING ON GOD

THE LORD WILL FIGHT FOR YOU; YOU NEED ONLY TO BE STILL." - EXODUS 14:14 NIV

When we are going through emotional pain, it's common to keep ourselves occupied with things to avoid feeling the pain. I can be the first to admit that I hate being still when I'm hurting. Whenever I have experienced a breakup or going through any grief, I've always tried to keep myself busy. I found it challenging to sit still and face the sadness in my heart. The healing process felt like it would never end, and each day felt like a never-ending cycle of despair. It was a feeling of hopelessness that greeted me each morning as soon as I woke up.

Heartbreak and grief can make us feel like we are in a battle that cannot be won. Unfortunately, it cannot be treated with medication or a band-aid, like physical injuries or illnesses. Emotional pain is internal and not easily cured. This can leave us feeling hopeless and defeated, as the recovery process does not have a specific timeline. The most challenging part is not knowing how long it will take to heal and what life will be like afterward. The uncertainty can be the most difficult part of the process.

Exodus 14:14 is a comforting Bible verse that assures us that God promises to fight for us, and all we have to do is be still. A few months after my breakup, I woke up with 1414 on my mind. At that point, I hadn't started reading the Bible yet, so I did not recognize it as a Bible verse. I searched for it on Google to see if it was a Bible verse, and Exodus 14:14 popped up. I remember crying because it was exactly what I needed to hear at that moment. It gave me a sense of peace and comfort because I knew God put that number on my mind for a reason so I could learn one of the ways He speaks.

No matter how big our battles are, God's Word is our weapon. You don't have to figure out how to defeat this battle alone. God has promised to fight for you, so all you have to do is step back and let Him take the lead. When I stopped trying to figure everything out and surrendered it all to God, I started to feel stronger day by day. Before I read this verse, I had tried everything to heal myself. I paid for all sorts of courses and books on how to get over a breakup, but it didn't last long before I ended up feeling the same as I did before.

When I started asking God to heal me, everything changed. Although therapy, courses, books, and other resources can be helpful, they are not the ultimate source of healing. God is the ultimate healer, and He can turn heartbreak into happiness much quicker than any breakup course or book can. When God tells us to be still, there is an opportunity for Him to speak to us. We can't hear from God when we're constantly keeping ourselves busy. God is our Heavenly Father and wants to take care of us. Therefore, we should take our hands off the wheel and let Him fight this battle for us.

REFLECT/JOURNAL

Take a moment to reflect on the times when God has proven to be faithful to you in the past. What are some of those moments? Write them down. In what area of your life do you need God to fight for you? How can you incorporate more stillness into your life? It is essential to take some time every day to sit in silence and ask God to speak to you.

PRAYER

Dear Heavenly Father, Your Word promises that You will fight for me. You see the heartbreak and pain I am going through right now, and I need You. I know this battle is not mine to fight, and I trust that I can rest and put it in Your hands. I can't do this on my own, and I need Your strength. Please comfort me when I am hurting and remind me I can rest knowing what Your Word says. I trust that You will help me fight this battle even when I can't see or feel it. In Jesus' name, Amen.

Day 24: Strength for a Weary Soul

But those who trust in the LORD will renew their strength; they will soar on wings like eagles; they will run and not become weary, they will walk and not faint. - Isaiah 40:31 CSB

God's Word is not just a collection of promises, but a direct communication from Him to us. He wants us to understand that our strength is not self-generated, but a gift from Him. As long as we stay connected to Him, He is the power source that keeps us going. So, how do we tap into this divine strength? We do so by waiting and trusting in Him, not relying on our limited strength and willpower.

Waiting on the Lord is not a passive act but an active pursuit of His strength. He promises to rejuvenate the strength of those who trust in Him, enabling us to soar on wings like eagles. He compares the strength He bestows upon us to that of an eagle, a creature known for its power and majesty. With God's strength, we can rise above any obstacle, running without growing weary.

This supernatural strength sustains us even in our weakest moments, carrying us forward.

I remember a time when I felt so overwhelmed with weariness that I didn't even have the energy to worship or pray; even that seemed to take too much out of me. But then I remembered this verse, got on my knees to pray, and spoke it out loud to God, asking Him to renew my strength. While I prayed, I struggled to get the words out because I couldn't stop crying and felt emotionally defeated and drained. I was tired of fighting and feeling like every day was a struggle.

After I finished praying, I still felt weak, but I decided to go for a trail walk outside and get some fresh air. As soon as I started towards the trail, I felt immediately exhausted and needed to sit down. I saw a bench far off to the side, so I walked over to sit down. As I was about to sit down, what was engraved on the bench caught my eye. It was this exact verse—Isaiah 40:31.

Immediately, I was strengthened and filled with joy, knowing that God had guided me to that bench. The memory of that moment still brings a smile to my face. Despite being tired and weak, I felt a supernatural strength and energy to walk the trail after that encounter. It was a God moment, and I realized He had led me to that specific bench to strengthen me. None of the other benches in the park had Bible verses on them; only the one I sat on did. When we ask God to strengthen us, we can wait expectantly for Him to show up. His words are not just there to make us feel better; His words hold power. We can trust what His Word says in the Bible because there is power and truth in it, and we can rely on it to face life's challenges. It is our sword to fight back and overcome.

God delights in us when we quote scripture and speak His Word back to Him in prayer. For instance, I often say, "God, in Isaiah 40:31, You promise to renew my strength and mount me up on wings like an eagle. I trust in Your Word and seek Your strength in this situation." By finding a scripture that resonates with our specific circumstances and incorporating it into our prayers, we can effectively apply the wisdom of the Bible to our lives. The Bible offers a solution to every challenge we encounter; we just need to search for them and put them into practice.

REFLECT/JOURNAL

Identify the areas where you feel weak and ask God to strengthen you. You can do this by speaking this verse back to Him in prayer and asking for His help. Tell Him where you need His strength, and then wait for Him to show up. Consider finding other Bible verses that speak to your situation and recite them back to Him. Write all of these down so you can have something to return to in prayer. This will show Him that you trust in His Word and are seeking His help. Wait and trust that He will give you the strength and guidance you need.

PRAYER

Dear Heavenly Father, Your strength is truly incredible. I am so thankful that I do not have to rely on my own strength. Even when I am weak, please help me to trust that You are the source of my strength. I pray that You give me the endurance to keep going and help me to overcome the battles I face. Help me to wait on You so that my strength will be renewed, and that I will not become weary. In Jesus' name, Amen.

Day 25: It Will All Be Worth It

Consider it pure joy, my brothers and sisters, whenever you face trials of many kinds, because you know that the testing of your faith produces perseverance. Let perseverance finish its work so that you may be mature and complete, not lacking anything. - James 1:2-4 NIV

How can going through trials be considered joy? *God, don't you understand how painful this is? Why would I even think of considering this as joy? I'm hurting God, and I definitely don't feel joyful right now.* However, James tells us that we can count our trials as joy because it produces something in us. As painful as they may be, our trials are not in vain. They strengthen us, and the testing of our faith produces endurance. God uses our suffering and trials to produce something worthwhile and eternal. Our suffering isn't pointless, and God uses all of it to produce spiritual maturity. Your suffering wasn't for nothing. When we face trials, our faith gets tested, and through that testing, is what produces perseverance.

Heartbreak is an inevitable part of our lives that we cannot avoid. We can't dodge that kind of bullet from happening. At some point in our lives, it will happen to us, whether it be from a relationship, divorce, loss of a loved one, loss of a job, or betrayal. Suffering is a part of the human experience, which, unfortunately, we cannot escape. As James said, we will face trials of many kinds, and it is not a matter of *if*, but *when*.

Nevertheless, we can find encouragement in these verses from scripture and learn to count our trials as joy because they produce patience and endurance in us. Through our trials, we learn that we can overcome all things through Christ, who gives us strength to endure. God uses our trials to make us steadfast and more resilient. God tests our faith by allowing us to go through trials. These trials reveal the true extent of our faith and determine where we have placed our trust.

Have we put our faith in our relationships, finances, or spouse? Even though God already knows the level of our faith, the trials we face expose the level of our faith to ourselves. When I went through my painful breakup, it revealed to me that I had placed all my faith in my relationship instead of God. My foundation was not built on Christ but on my relationship, and my emotions depended on my circumstances. When the breakup happened, it devastated me because I had nothing left to put my faith in. When my relationship ended, my faith went with it. However, this painful experience led me into the arms of Jesus, where I found real hope that I could cling to.

This experience has taught me a valuable lesson: we should not put our faith in someone or something that can quickly be taken away from us at any moment. Instead, we should build our faith on God and God alone. By doing so, we will have a strong foundation that will keep us standing firm when storms come our way. Trials are a way to test our faith and reveal where we put our hope and trust. Each trial strengthens our faith and gives us more endurance for the next one. As we overcome each trial, we become stronger and more spiritually mature. Ultimately, we see that every trial has produced perseverance in us.

Consider the trials we face to lifting weights at the gym. If you've never worked out before, you wouldn't be able to lift heavy weights right away. You would have to start with lighter ones and gradually increase the weight to avoid injury. Over time, your muscles and endurance are built and trained to handle heavier weights. Similarly, the trials we face are like a spiritual workout. They help us develop our inner strength and endurance. God uses these trials to train us, preparing us to face even greater challenges in the future.

We can find joy in the midst of our trials because we know that God is working on our behalf. God doesn't allow us to go through hardship for no reason. He allows us to face trials so we can become stronger and better than we were before. For this reason, James encourages us to find joy in our trials - not because they are enjoyable, but because they allow us to grow and mature. Trials enable us to rely more on God, allowing Him to shape and mold us into becoming who He created for us to be.

REFLECT/JOURNAL

In the midst of heartbreak, take a moment to reflect on how your faith has been strengthened. Perhaps you have found comfort in prayer or turned to your community for support. Whatever the case may be, it's important to acknowledge the ways in which your faith can be strengthened during difficult times. As you deal with this trial, keep in mind that you have the power to choose how you react. Are you responding to this trial with unbelief and complaining, or are you viewing it as an opportunity to grow? What kind of endurance is your heartbreak producing in you, and how has your faith been strengthened?

PRAYER

Dear Heavenly Father, I feel overwhelmed with

grief due to this heartbreak. I humbly ask for Your guidance to help me change the way I perceive this trial. Please grant me a steadfast spirit so that I can walk through this difficult time with grace. I pray that You use this heartbreak to produce an endurance within me so that I may persevere and come out of this situation stronger. I also pray that my dependence on You increases and that I put my hope and trust in You, Lord, rather than in my circumstances. In Jesus' name, Amen.

Day 26: Faith in the Unseen

Now faith is confidence in what we hope for and assurance about what we do not see. - Hebrews 11:1 NIV

Just like our physical eyesight is evidence of what we see in the physical, faith works the same way as evidence for the things in the spiritual. I'm sure you've heard the expression, "I'll believe it when I see it," but that's not having faith; that's having proof. There would be no use for faith if you could already see it. Faith is only needed when you hope or believe for the things you have not yet seen. Faith says, "I'll see it when I believe it."

Faith is having confidence in what we have yet to see or experience. It means that we trust and hold onto something that we believe to be true, even when we have no physical proof. We cannot physically see Jesus, but we can feel His presence because we believe in Him. Those who don't believe in Jesus cannot experience the same things we do. Our faith opens doors for Jesus to move and work in our lives. Jesus Himself said that He could not perform miracles in His own hometown because of their lack of faith (Mark 6:5-6).

As you can see, faith is essential in the Kingdom of God. It shapes our perspective and guides our actions. Our belief system influences our lives and determines the choices we make. In our spiritual journey, we need faith to rely on God even when we can't understand His ways. Faith means accepting God's words and holding on to His promises. When God says He knows the plans He has for us and that He works all things together for our good, we must trust in His words and believe them to be true.

God loves when we have child-like faith. It pleases Him to see us put our complete trust in His plan and surrender our need to control or understand everything. When I went through my breakup, I clung to many of the Bible verses you now read in this devotional. Despite having no proof that things would get better, I wrote down these verses in my journal and prayed them over myself for comfort. Often, on the same day, I would see the same verses appearing at places I went, which comforted me to know that God was with me and always listening.

Months after my breakup, I realized that God was truly reshaping and transforming me. The emotional pain gradually subsided, and I stopped crying myself to sleep. I kept seeing signs that said "faith over fear," which encouraged me to keep going. Having faith can truly shift the way we live. Even in times of pain, God will stretch our faith to show us His power. There is always a purpose in the pain, and oftentimes, God uses heartbreak to bring our focus back to Him so that He can strengthen our faith. That is exactly what happened to me, and I wouldn't change a thing. I am grateful for my heartbreak because it brought me closer to God and gave me an unshakeable faith.

REFLECT/JOURNAL

The way we perceive things determines our response to them. Are you viewing things from a place of belief or solely based on your circumstances? Do you have faith that God has a purpose for the pain you are experiencing? Are you willing to trust that God will use everything for your good? Do you believe what God says in His Word? If you find it difficult to trust God or believe these things, ask God to help you overcome your doubts and examine why you struggle to trust Him.

PRAYER

Dear Heavenly Father, I thank You for Your Word that I can cling to when I feel hopeless. Thank You for Your comfort and encouragement. Thank You for Your promises that I can rely on when I start to doubt. Lord, please strengthen my faith and help me with any unbelief that I may have in my heart. Please guide me to trust You wholeheartedly, even when I am hurting. Please provide me with encouragement and support, Lord, as I go about my day. In Jesus' name, Amen.

Day 27: Focus on God

But seek first the kingdom of God and his righteousness, and all these things will be added to you. - Matthew 6:33 ESV

When I first came across this verse and learned what it meant, I wondered if it was really that easy. Would everything be added to me if I just sought God? The answer is yes; it really is that simple. Every day, we are bombarded with worries and anxieties about things we cannot control. However, God doesn't want us to worry about how or when things will happen. He knows what we need and wants us to keep our focus on Him instead of worrying. When we seek Him first, everything else falls into place, and we can be assured that God will take care of the rest.

God is sovereign, which means He has complete control over everything. He is ultimately The One in charge of making things happen when they need to happen. This verse encourages us to focus on the Kingdom of God and let Him take care of everything else. Although God knows our deepest desires, wants, and needs, we should not prioritize those things over the things of God. If you make God your first priority, He will take care of everything else, including your heartbreak.

When I was going through my breakup, I felt so broken and lost. I honestly felt like I was a lost cause to be going through another heartbreak in my early thirties and still not married with kids like all my other friends were at that point. I had all these goals and dreams that I wanted to accomplish. Yet, here I was at rock bottom again, crying over another failed relationship. I couldn't concentrate on anything else except the pain of my emotions and wondering when it would all end. I think it hurt even more because of the focus I put on my age. I had to start all over again and felt so behind in life. The good news, though, is that I was starting over with God this time – something I had never done before.

God allowed my heart to get broken because He knew it would teach me an eternal lesson that would benefit me forever. God might be doing the same thing in your life through your heartbreak. In my previous breakups, I never sought God long enough for Him to heal me; I wanted a quick fix. Instead, I tried to numb my pain with things of the world, like partying, drinking, and trying to find the next guy. I never gave God my time or total commitment.

I still prayed and went to church every so often, but I never sought God or included Him in the plans for my life. I made all my decisions independently and never asked God's permission or His thoughts for what I desired. I had no idea there was a difference between our own will and God's will for our lives. When God wouldn't answer my prayers fast enough, I gave up on seeking Him altogether and only turned to Him in times of need. This is where many of us make a mistake. We give up too quickly before allowing God to intervene in our situation.

The pain of my breakup led me to turn to God with a renewed commitment that I never had before. Before this, I had never opened my Bible or truly understood what it meant to seek God. As I began to seek God and His will, I started to grasp the significance of putting Him first. I began to read the Bible regularly and listen to sermons instead of watching Netflix before bedtime. The more I continued to seek God, the more my heartbreak began to dissipate because I had a greater desire to focus on God than on my pain.

I can now fully grasp the concept of what this verse means. All the desires I once had turned out to be completely different once I got to know God and His will for my life. Letting our emotions guide us can be dangerous, as the famous saying, 'follow your heart' is misleading. The Bible clearly states the heart is deceitful above all things, and only God knows the heart (Jeremiah 17:9). God knows what we need far more than we do. Therefore, it is essential to focus on God and His will for our lives and let Him take care of everything else. Matthew 6:33 promises that everything else will fall into place if we seek God's Kingdom first. I can testify that this is true.

REFLECT/JOURNAL

God has a perfect plan for each of our lives, but He gives us the freedom to choose whether to follow His plan or our own path. If you want to know God's will for your life, start by writing down your dreams and desires. Then, ask God if they align with His will. Seek the kingdom of God first, and He will guide you and give you the desires of your heart. Remember, God is a gentleman, and He only guides those who are willing to be led by Him.

PRAYER

Dear Heavenly Father, I am amazed by Your sovereignty and power. Thank You for being a compassionate and loving Father who understands my needs. As I go through this challenging time, please help me to seek Your guidance and will for my life. I only want what You want for me, so please guide me on the right path. Teach me to do Your will and help give me the desires of my heart. I trust that as long as I keep my focus on You, You will take care of everything else. In Jesus' name, Amen.

Day 28: A Changed Heart

Delight yourself in the LORD, and he will give you the desires of your heart. - Psalm 37:4 ESV

I recognize that it can be challenging to place your trust in God when you find yourself in a seemingly hopeless situation. I can deeply relate to how you feel and what you are going through. I have been in your shoes many times, most recently just a year and a half ago, as I write this devotional. I know the intense pain that fills your heart and the restlessness you feel. As someone who has experienced similar struggles, I want to encourage you with this Psalm. Instead of allowing worry to consume you, I urge you to redirect your emotions towards God. Psalm 37:4 tells us that when we delight in the Lord, He will give us our hearts' desires. You might be wondering, *how does this relate to heartbreak or my current situation?*

When we experience emotional pain, our perception of situations can become skewed. Our pain can distort our perspective, making it difficult to see the situation for what it truly is; it's like looking through a cracked and distorted lens. However, if we were to view it from God's perspective, we would realize that it's not as we perceive it. When we are not in harmony with God's will, our hearts' desires do not align with His but rather our own. We may later come to understand that what we perceived as a setback was actually an opportunity for growth and maturity. Sometimes, the end of a relationship is what paves the way for a breakthrough. In fact, the breakup may be God's way of redirecting us so that we can realign with His will.

Before I started seeking God's guidance for all my life decisions, I used to choose my partners and the qualities I *thought* I wanted. I always went for the same types of guys who possessed similar traits and qualities. I had a checklist of everything I wanted my future husband to have. However, every relationship I had ended the same way. I couldn't help but wonder if there was something wrong with my taste in men or if it was my list. In reality, the main reason behind my failed relationships was that I wasn't seeking God's approval in my choices and didn't have a close relationship with Him. After ending my last relationship, I gave up on my list because it wasn't getting me anywhere, and I didn't want to date someone similar to my previous partners. Eventually, I realized that the problem wasn't my list but my relationship with Jesus.

I idolized being in love so badly that it pulled me into the wrong relationships. I was starving for love, which resulted in me accepting anything that "seemed" good enough, even if it wasn't healthy or what I knew I deserved. But as I grew closer to God, my desires started to change. I no longer found myself attracted to the same type of people I used to date. It truly shocked me to look back at what I was once attracted to and put up with once I got closer to God. My entire pallet changed. Psalm 37 promises that if we delight ourselves in the Lord, He will give us the desires of our hearts.

God longs to fulfill our hearts' desires if they align with His will. To understand God's desires for us, we need to have a close relationship with Him. This means spending time with Him in prayer and studying in the Word. The more we seek God, our tastes and desires change, and our hearts are transformed. We realize that true satisfaction comes from the Lord, not from worldly pursuits or relationships. God completely changed my tastes and desires for everything, including my hobbies. Who I was in past relationships and who I am now are two different people. God will do the same for you. If you seek God with all your heart, He will change your desires and put new ones in you.

REFLECT/JOURNAL

Reflect on the deepest desires of your heart. What are your heart's desires? Do these desires align with God's will for your life? If you're uncertain, ask

God for guidance and clarity. Consider whether your desires honor God or simply serve yourself. Write down your heart's desires and ask God to align them with His will.

PRAYER

Dear Heavenly Father, You know the deepest desires of my heart and the hopes and dreams I have for the future. I ask that You grant me the desires of my heart, so that I may align with Your will for my life. If I have any desires that do not align with Your will, I ask that You take those desires away. Please continue to guide me in the direction of my purpose and dreams, and reveal to me my calling. I pray that my desires align with Yours as I continue to seek Your will for my life. In Jesus' name, Amen.

Day 29: It Will All Make Sense

Jesus replied, "You do not realize now what I am doing, but later you will understand." - John 13:7 NIV

When we feel broken, it can feel like nothing in our life makes any sense. *What was the point of it all?* If you are anything like me, you must know the purpose behind everything. However, there are certain things in life we aren't meant to understand, but that doesn't mean they are purposeless. This verse reminds us that at the right time, God will reveal to us why things had to happen a certain way. There have been many instances in my life where I have wondered why certain things happened the way they did. At the time, I didn't understand the reason behind them. But later on, when I looked back, I could see God's greater plan and purpose in it all.

Heartbreak may seem unbearable, but it can be one of God's most powerful experiences He uses to transform us. Through the pain and heartbreak, God shapes and molds us into the person He intended for us to be. As we allow Him to heal us, He purifies our hearts, develops our character, and eliminates any impurities that may hinder us from reaching our full potential. When the time is right, God will bring clarity and understanding to your situation, just like He did with the disciples in John 13:7. They didn't understand the significance of Jesus washing their feet until later. There was a much deeper work and meaning than just the disciples' feet being washed. Similarly, God is doing a deeper, spiritual, and emotional cleansing in you through this heartbreak. He is cleansing you in ways you might not understand yet, but it's all part of His plan to transform you into the person He created you to be.

You will soon see the purpose of this heartbreak. While going through mine, I couldn't see one positive thing it could bring me. It was the worst pain I have ever felt, and some days, I really felt like I was dying. A few months into the healing process, God started revealing things to me about the purpose of it. He showed me how I had never healed properly from my past breakups. I had put bandaids on all of my wounds and went into the next relationship with the baggage from the previous one. God used my most painful breakup to finally heal me from the inside out.

The healing process I went through this time was different from all my previous experiences. I learned a valuable lesson – that God never allows us to skip tests and will continue to give us the same test until we pass it. In the past, I jumped from one toxic relationship to another, hoping to fill the emptiness in my heart through them. But after several failed relationships, I finally understood that only God can fill the void in our hearts. I was looking for love in all the wrong places. God's love is the only love that can truly fulfill us and make us feel whole. Once I realized this, I was able to address the root cause of my problem and heal the wounds that kept me stuck in the same cycle.

Many of us hold onto things past their expiration date in fear of abandonment. Our childhood can affect how we show up in our adult relationships. For me, my Dad left when I was little, and ever since then, I tried to heal that abandonment wound in all my romantic relationships. As a result, I sought out relationships and partners that I could fix. I thought if I could fix something in someone else, it would fill the void I had from my Dad. I never turned to God for help; instead, I turned to alcohol, work, and men.

Going through such a traumatic breakup in my early thirties made me desperate for change. The day I called out to God to save me from my pain, He showed up right on the scene. I finally looked to the right place for help instead of another drink or dating app. In hindsight, all those lessons led me straight to the Helper I never knew I needed - God. If it weren't for all those failed relationships, I would have never been in such a desperate place to seek God for change. Nothing we go through is ever wasted. God knows exactly what He's doing in your life. It might not make sense right now, but just like the disciples, you, too, will look back and understand the purpose and meaning behind it. It will all make sense one day.

REFLECT/JOURNAL

What lessons do you think God is trying to teach you during this season of heartbreak? What resonated with you in this devotional and gave you some confirmation or clarity about your own situation? Take some time to reflect and ask God to reveal the lessons He is trying to teach you through this. In a few months, you will be able to come back to this journal entry and have a better understanding of the purpose behind it.

PRAYER

Dear Heavenly Father, thank You for always knowing what I need, even before I ask You. Although I may not understand what You are doing in my life right now, I find comfort in Your Word that assures me that everything will make sense later. Please help me to heal from the pain of confusion that I am going through at the moment, and give me peace of mind, knowing that You are working it all out for my good. Father, please reveal the lessons that You are trying to teach me so I can learn from them and not repeat any cycles. I trust there is a purpose behind everything that I have had to go through. Thank You for being the best kind of teacher. In Jesus' name, Amen.

Day 30: God Will Finish the Work in You

I AM SURE OF THIS, THAT HE WHO STARTED A GOOD WORK IN YOU WILL CARRY IT ON TO COMPLETION UNTIL THE DAY OF CHRIST JESUS. - PHILIPPIANS 1:6 CSB

God always finishes what He starts, and His ultimate goal is to transform us into the image of Christ. Sometimes, He allows us to go through painful experiences, such as heartbreak, to shape us more into the image of Jesus. God uses our struggle and pain to draw us closer to Him. The pain we experience drives us to seek God more for healing and gets to the root cause of the issue - our hearts. Our brokenness draws us closer to God, and it is in our weakness that we experience God's power and strength the most.

God uses our pain to refine us. Just like gold refined through fire, we are refined through trials. For gold to achieve a higher level of purity, it must go through a higher-temperature flame. The purpose of the fire is to remove any impurities from the gold. The hotter the fire, the purer the gold. This gold-refining process is a metaphor for the life of a believer. Each trial we go through purifies us of any impurities that we may have. When we experience pain, the things in our hearts that need healing are exposed. Just as fire brings impurities of gold to the surface, our pain brings the impurities of our hearts to the surface. And this is where God's real work in us begins – removing the impurities.

God, the one who began a good work in you the day you became a born-again believer, promises to finish the work He started in you. Philippians 1:6 assures us that God will carry it to completion until the day of Christ Jesus. God is not a one-time transformer, but a continuous one. He is constantly transforming us and will continue to do so until He returns. To illustrate this, think of it like a puzzle. When you start a puzzle, you don't stop when you complete the outer edges; you continue it until completion. It's the same as when you buy a book; you don't purchase it to stop reading after the first chapter but to read it entirely. God's promise of continuous transformation gives us security and hope for our future.

God is the same with us. He doesn't start the work in us only to leave us unchanged; He continues what He started in us from day one. God will complete the transformation He began in us. We are the clay, and God is the potter, and He will finish the transformation He started within us until the day Jesus returns. The transformation talked about here is the process of sanctification. Through the sanctification process, we become more holy each day as we walk with the Lord. It doesn't happen overnight; it's a process that God promises to continue in us.

Through the pain of your aching heart, God is working to refine and transform your character. This process involves exposing and removing any impurities that may be present in your heart. The emotional turmoil that comes with heartbreak can feel like you're going through a fire, but it serves a purpose in revealing insecurities and wounds that may have been buried and unaddressed. It's not uncommon for past hurts to resurface during this time. Ever notice how all of your insecurities rise to the surface again after a breakup? Or the abandonment wounds you thought you healed from are now being triggered again? Relationships can cover up those wounds for a bit, but when a storm hits, the bandages fall off, exposing the deep wounds. Things you thought you were healed from were just dormant and asleep, but heartbreak exposes what's really hidden beneath the surface.

When we experience the pain of heartbreak, it can bring up unresolved traumas that we may have buried deep within ourselves. However, God's purpose isn't to leave you feeling broken, but to heal and purify your heart of any impurities. In this process, God is removing all the junk that's been stored up in your heart that hasn't been cleaned out properly from past hurts. Heartbreak might feel like you are in a fire, but when you come out, you won't be the same as when you went in; God is purifying you.

If you feel like you are going through the fire right now, know that you are being purified to be more like Jesus. He is cleaning and removing the impurities out of you and will finish the work He started in you. In this process, it's important to remember that healing takes time. It's not a linear journey, but a series of ups and downs. We can have faith and assurance that God will not leave us how He found us but to see the transformation to completion. God wants to fully restore your heart from the trauma that has been hiding beneath the surface. Remember that the pain will not last forever and that you will come out of it stronger and more resilient than before. The heartbreak has a purpose.

REFLECT/JOURNAL

What emotional wounds have resurfaced as a result of this heartbreak? These may include past traumas, insecurities, abandonment wounds, fears, or triggers. Can you pinpoint where these wounds first came from? How do you see God using this heartbreak to refine and purify you?

PRAYER

Dear Heavenly Father, thank You for the work that You have begun in me. Lord, I pray that You will continue transforming me and purifying my heart by removing all its impurities. Please help me to recognize any wounds that have been hidden beneath the surface and heal them. I ask that You peel back the layers so I can be fully restored and made new. Please shape and mold me to look more like You, Jesus. I trust that You will finish the work that You started in me. In Jesus' name, Amen.

Day 31: God is for You

What then shall we say to these things? If God is for us, who can be against us? - Romans 8:31 ESV

Romans 8:31 is a verse we can cling to when we go through trials and suffering. This verse should give us confidence that God is always on our side. We should find comfort in knowing that God is for us and not against us. As His children, we can trust that God wants only the best for us and does not enjoy seeing us suffer. Therefore, when we experience pain or hardship, we can trust that there is a good reason for it. Even when it seems like God is absent or against us, we must hold onto the truth that He is always for us. We can take heart in the fact that God has already made a way for us, and we can trust Him completely despite our pain and grief.

All the great men in the Bible were known for their sufferings and hardships. They all faced various trials and difficulties, but with God's help, they overcame them. It's worth noting that no great man in the Bible went through pain or suffering where God was not with them. Even when Israel was being disobedient,

God was still by their side. Joseph endured being sold as a slave and spent years in prison, but God never abandoned him. David was once overwhelmed with despair but found comfort in God's presence. God had a plan for their sufferings and used it all for their ultimate good.

The enemy's strategy is to draw a wedge between you and God when you go through difficult times. The devil desires for you to hold a grudge against God and turn away from Him. The enemy knows that if you turn away from God, then you will stop praying and seeking Him, which is his ultimate goal. The devil wants to destroy your faith because he knows that God is close to the brokenhearted and saves those crushed in spirit. The enemy knows the perfect time to attack is when you are in pain because you are weak and vulnerable. The devil desires for you to blame God and be angry at Him rather than coming to Him in prayer. This is why many turn away from God when bad things happen. The enemy manipulates their thoughts and snatches away their faith. The devil's plan is to get you to harden your heart towards God.

Whenever doubts start creeping in from the enemy, remind yourself that God is for you, not against you. Don't let the devil take away your faith. Even in the midst of trials and pain, remember that God is still good. You may not understand why you are going through this, but trust that God has a bigger plan and purpose for it. Praise God even in the pain. Worship is warfare that breaks things off in the spirit. Just like grapes must go through a crushing process to produce wine, we must go through trials to be conformed into the image of Christ. You may be in a crushing season right now, but God knows it is necessary for your spiritual growth and development.

God is rooting for your healing. God is rooting for your purpose. He is on your side and wants you to come out of this trial stronger than before. The purpose of your pain is not to leave you unchanged; it is to purify your heart, remove impurities, and mend all the broken pieces together so you can be made whole again. We must embrace the pain because God has a plan for us. As Hebrews 12:6 states, "For the Lord disciplines the one he loves." Although God does not cause heartbreak or pain, He can use difficult times to draw us closer to Him. Always remember that God is for us, not against us; Jeremiah 29:11 tells us that He has good plans for us.

Knowing that God is for us should bring a deep sense of comfort, assuring us that the suffering we experience is not the end. He did not bring you here to abandon you but to guide you through it all. No matter what hardships you may face, you can be sure that the love of the Father will never, ever leave you. He is always by your side, unwavering and steadfast. Remember, after every storm comes a rainbow. There is glory waiting for you on the other side, and brighter and better days are ahead.

REFLECT/JOURNAL

How can you feel God's presence with you in your pain? Have you experienced any moments when God reminded you that He was by your side? God speaks and comforts those who are brokenhearted; we just need to be open to the ways He reveals Himself to us. How has God shown Himself to you? I encourage you to look for the ways in which God speaks to you today. He is present even in the smallest details.

PRAYER

Dear Heavenly Father, thank You for always being for me and with me. Your Word gives me comfort and encouragement to know You are on my side. Please help remind me of this when I feel weak and hopeless. I don't always understand why I go through the things I do, but I know that if You are for me, then I have no reason to fear. I trust that You are working in my life and will bring me out better than before. Thank You, Father, for always looking out for me. In Jesus' name, Amen.

About the Author

Alicia Cummings is a Christian author, influencer, and certified relationship coach/mentor. She is passionate about sharing her testimony on social media after experiencing a toxic relationship herself. Alicia is now dedicated to helping others heal from heartbreak and helping them find their God-given purpose and destiny. Her mission is to use the gifts that God has given her to heal, inspire, and encourage others around the world to become who God has called them to be.

For more information visit:
www.aliciacummings.com

Connect with Alicia on social media:

Instagram: @aliciacummings
TikTok: @aliciacummings11
YouTube: @aliciacummings

Made in the USA
Coppell, TX
08 February 2025

45632656R00089